T0248969

# "Europe" in the Middle Ages

# PAST IMPERFECT

**See further**
www.arc-humanities.org/our-series/pi

# "Europe" in the Middle Ages

### Klaus Oschema

**British Library Cataloguing in Publication Data**
A catalogue record for this book is available from the British Library

ISBN (print) 9781641891592
e-ISBN (PDF) 9781802701357
e-ISBN (EPUB) 9781802701364

**www.arc-humanities.org**
Printed and bound in the UK (by CPI Group [UK] Ltd), USA (by Bookmasters),
and elsewhere using print-on-demand technology.

# Contents

# List of Illustrations

# Preface and Acknowledgements

For a medievalist who lives and works in the early twenty-first century, writing about Europe is a highly ambivalent undertaking. Some readers might be tempted to argue that the topic hardly merits our attention, since they consider the medieval evidence too sparse or too inconclusive. Others might think that the choice of subject constitutes *per se* an unwelcome relapse into Eurocentric tendencies. In any case, it seems clear that the subject inevitably evokes current political debates. Whether one subscribes to the conviction that Europe merits becoming the framework for an increasingly interconnected and profound political and cultural community or, to the contrary, clings to the, historically speaking, relatively new belief that people are best organized in the form of nation-states, talking about Europe has political overtones.

Having studied the use of the notion of Europe for quite some time now, I am very conscious about these effects. It might thus be helpful to clarify my own position: Born and raised in late twentieth-century Germany, I was seventeen years old when the Berlin wall fell. I grew up to be deeply convinced that the European Union (EU) constitutes a vital means of overcoming the numerous problems that the nation-state entails—and I still stand by these convictions. As an historian, however, I am also convinced that political questions and problems cannot be solved by looking backwards: history does not furnish ready-made answers. What it can do, is provide alternative perspectives and information that helps us to better understand our problems in the first place. What we choose to do remains our own responsibility.

In this sense, I would like to stress that the material and the interpretations I present in this little book should neither be read as an affirmation of current EU-policies—nor as their rejection. My work as an historian focuses on analyzing and understanding how people used the notion of Europe in the medieval past and which ideas they connected with that term. I can see no convincing argument that would force us to accept that the phenomena we can see here determine or justify any specific modern interpretation of "Europe".

That said, I would like to thank the staff at Arc Humanities Press for inviting me to write this short book, which largely relies on a (far too voluminous) study I published in German exactly a decade ago. I am indebted to Simon Forde for his detailed feedback on the original manuscript—and particularly to Angela Roberts (Manchester) for her invaluable work on the "denglish" first version. Whenever anything sounds like idiomatic English, it's thanks to her efforts and those of my wonderful colleague and long-time friend Chris Jones (Christchurch, Aotearoa/New Zealand). I am also grateful to the anonymous reviewer for helping me to eliminate a number of shortcomings. My wife Monica Corrado also read the text and pointed out several problems—but she obviously deserves my gratitude for much more that than. Finally, my thanks go out to Patrick Geary, who taught me more than he'll probably realize.

Chapter I

# Why Europe? A Concept Crossing History and Politics

The title of this short monograph merits explanation. Although the name "Europe" has enjoyed immense popularity in medieval studies from the mid-twentieth century onwards, it is by no means obvious what an analysis of "'Europe' in the Middle Ages" might comprise. What's more, the use of the term in medieval studies is far from obvious, as we shall see. On the most general level, recent publications on "Europe in the Middle Ages" can be divided into two categories: the majority seek to describe events and developments that took place in the geographical unit that we now identify as "Europe." Sometimes they analyze and identify the formation of what is often called a "European culture"[1] or even a "European identity."

Another series of studies, smaller in number, focuses on the development of the concept (or the idea) of Europe. They do not so much ask "What happened in Europe during the Middle Ages?" or "What were the characteristics of medieval societies in Europe?," but instead focus on whether the *notion*

---

[1] See Bartlett, *Making of Europe*. For the sake of brevity and due to the introductory character of this short book, I will limit the references as far as possible. The contributions that can be found in the bibliography will be quoted with short titles. Direct quotations from sources that are given without references can conveniently be identified online (OA) in Oschema, *Bilder von Europa* (see bibliography; references will be given with the abbreviation *BE*, followed by the page number).

(or a *concept*) of Europe played a role during the period we call the Middle Ages and how this role can be described.

It is the historians' role to probe sources for answers—but the questions they choose to ask are inevitably informed by the present day. Many authors have searched for the "roots" of the idea of European political unity in the Middle Ages, but the first historians to do so, from the late 1940s onwards, were somewhat disappointed by what they found. Around 1990, when the fall of the Berlin Wall sparked renewed interest in all questions concerning the history and identity of "Europe," medievalists began synthesizing the findings of these pioneering works. They asserted that the word "Europe" was used quite rarely in the medieval period and that it remained a "purely geographical" notion for most of the time between the fifth and the fifteenth centuries.[2]

In the following pages I will argue that both assumptions are distorted, if not wrong. In order to make a convincing case for the modification of this well-established picture, I would have to present the available sources in much more detail than is possible in this book. To compensate for this unavoidable constraint, I direct interested readers to my longer monograph on the subject (*Bilder von Europa im Mittelalter*).

My initial remarks will have made clear that "Why Europe?" is an important question. While the subject is not an obvious one from a medievalist's perspective, the question can be answered in several ways. Based on what was, until quite recently, the mainstream of medieval research, one might argue that given the (alleged) scarcity and insignificance of the notion of Europe in medieval sources it is no subject at all. However, the question is also important for our own present, not least because we have learned about the perilous effects of Eurocentrism and the need to globalize perspectives if we want to create an adequate picture of the world we inhabit. In 2002, when Michael Mitterauer asked *Why Europe?*, he justified his endeavour by attempting to establish the medie-

---

**2** For a well-informed and concise overview from this period see Hiestand, "'Europa' im Mittelalter".

val roots of European hegemony in the modern period. His approach relied on the assumption that some specific features of European culture and environment laid the groundwork for developments that led to a kind of globalization of Europe.

Such an approach raises questions that must be analyzed, especially since the underlying master narrative of the "Europeanization of the World" has been shown to be highly problematic. My aim here is more limited. I believe that many of the discussions about the "nature" or the "essence" of Europe that still linger in scholarly discourse (and also in political debates, for instance in the media) are relatively impressionistic and based on highly subjective interpretations and ideas. It is hard to gauge whether the widespread Christianization of the part of world we call Europe made this particular religious feature a permanent part of "European identity," or whether it constitutes a contingent (and currently precarious) historical development. If the latter, does it make any sense to continue speaking of "Christian Europe" today? Analogous arguments could be made for other cultural features, such as the importance of cities and urban culture, the development of chivalry and knighthood, and so on.[3]

Instead of engaging with questions concerning the "Europeanness" of individual cultural traits and their historical development, I propose to merely trace the use of the word: Where and when did premodern authors employ the notion of "Europe"? What did they mean by it? Which further ideas and connotations became attached to it?

This book will not try to explain what Europe "really is" by looking either at earlier uses of the word or at phenomena that occurred in the space we identify as "Europe" today.

---

[3] For a list of features that characterized medieval "European" culture, see Heimpel, "Europa." Agnes Heller, "Europe: An Epilogue?," in *The Idea of Europe. Problems of National and Transnational Identity*, ed. Brian Nelson, David Roberts, and Walter Veit (Oxford: Berg, 1992), 12–25 at 14, plainly states "there is no European culture," declaring the respective models to be constructed in retrospect.

Instead, it will discuss a genuinely historical question by following the uses of the word through the period we call the "Middle Ages."

## Contemporary Expectations and the Quest for Historical Roots

These introductory remarks show that the analysis of ideas and "images" (in the loose sense of both physical and mental representations) of Europe in the Middle Ages is not self-evident. Until the mid-twentieth century, most historians of the Middle Ages were not particularly interested in Europe as a category of analysis. They rather searched for the roots of their own nation in the period that followed the so-called fall of the Roman Empire (what historians now prefer to describe as the "transformation of the Roman world").[4] In the nineteenth century, medieval history occupied an important role, mostly due to its political relevance in the endeavour to legitimize the modern nation-states by means of their history. Authors who referred to Europe when they reflected on medieval history were mostly philosophers: Friedrich Schlegel, for example, presented Charlemagne as a foundational figure in a "new Europe" (*BE* 38). Historians, on the other hand, mostly presented this Frankish king and Roman emperor in terms of national belonging. In this respect, the German historian Leopold von Ranke seems an exception at first glance, but a closer look reveals that his use of "Europe" mostly follows modern geographic conventions. Whenever his analyses developed more "universal" perspectives, he preferred to distinguish between "occidental" and "oriental" characteristics (*BE* 39–40).

After the experiences of the two World Wars, historians were equally influenced by the needs and discourse of their own time when searching for "Europe in the Middle Ages." In doing so, however, they rarely made their political inspiration

---

**4** For nineteenth-century approaches, see Geary, *The Myth of Nations*; for the "transformation" see the series "The Transformation of the Roman World" (since 2008: "Brill's Series on the Early Middle Ages").

explicit. It remains noticeable that the first studies to scruti-
nize the origins of an "occidental" sense of belonging, as well
as the relationship between Christianity and Europe from the
Middle Ages onwards, appeared only a few years after the
end of the First World War (BE 42–43: Richard Wallach, 1928;
Werner Fritzemeyer, 1931). One of the first medievalists to
explicitly emphasize the notion of Europe as a meaningful
cultural unit with long-standing effects, was Christopher
Dawson, an English Catholic, who identified the Carolingian
Empire as the nucleus of what he called the "true Europe."
Dawson's *Making of Europe* was soon translated into German—and the fact that his German publisher replaced the
continent's name in the title with "Occident" (*Abendland*)
expresses how marginal "Europe" was perceived to be in the
discussion of medieval subjects.[5]

This changed profoundly after the Second World War—or
more precisely, during the war's last years: by 1942, representatives of the Allies had already started planning the publication of a new history of Europe. This collective work was
meant to provide an "objective" history that would establish
the enduring development of a European culture. *The European Inheritance* was finally published in three volumes in
1954 (after a series of problems, due to the growing tensions
between the Allies),[6] and its obvious goal was to accentuate
a shared European culture after the trauma of conflict. This

---

**5** Dawson, *Making of Europe*; cf. Brigitte Leucht, "Christopher
Dawson (1889–1970)," in *Europa-Historiker*, 2:211–29. W. H. Roobol,
"Europe in the Historiograpy between the World Wars," in *Europe
from a Cultural Perspective. Historiography and Perceptions*, ed. Albert
Rijksbaron, W. H. Roobol, and M. Weisglas (The Hague: Nijgh en Van
Ditmar, 1987), 52–61 at 58–60, demonstrates that historians of the
modern period integrated the notion earlier than medievalists.

**6** *The European Inheritance*, ed. Ernest Barker, George Clarke, and
Paul Vaucher, 3 vols. (Oxford: Clarendon, 1954), 1:v; cf. Stuart
Woolf, "Europa und seine Historiker," in *Probleme und Perspektiven der
Europa-Historiographie*, ed. Hannes Siegrist and Rolf Petri, Comparativ
14/3 (Leipzig: Universitätsverlag, 2004), 50–71 at 55–56.

approach was not exceptional: the last years of the war (and those that immediately followed) witnessed the publication of an impressive series of pertinent studies by Federico Chabod and Carlo Curcio in Italy; Heinz Gollwitzer, Hermann Heimpel, and Jürgen Fischer in Germany; Oskar Halecki (a Pole who lived in exile in the United States); Bernard Voyenne and Lucien Febvre in France; and Denys Hay in Scotland. Much of their work focused on the notion and the idea of Europe in the Middle Ages and/or the early modern period. Together, these pioneering studies furnished the basis for later research.

Soon after the war, the notion of Europe, sometimes also the "Occident," became a concept that allowed historians to overcome categories which had been discredited (e.g., the "nation," especially from a German perspective) but simultaneously connected them to the political discourse. Reconstruction after the Second World War soon unfolded under "European" auspices: in 1950, the famous "Karlspreis" (Charlemagne Prize) was awarded for the first time (to Richard Coudenhove-Kalergi, the founder of the Paneuropean Union). With this prize, the German city of Aachen proposed to decorate individuals (and later also institutions) that had furthered the peaceful integration of Western Europe, thereby successfully claiming the notion of Europe for the Western, non-communist parts of the continent. At the same time, several "European" organizations that focused on economic and infrastructural questions were established, in order to ensure concrete political cooperation. After the formation of the Council of Europe (1949), the six nations of France, Germany, Italy, Belgium, the Netherlands, and Luxemburg created the European Community for Coal and Steel (1952) and soon deepened their cooperation with the European Economic Community and Euratom (1958; the Treaties of Rome were signed in 1957).[7]

In this situation, working on Europe gave medievalists a way to make a meaningful contribution to ongoing debates and developments, while also enabling the replacement

---

**7** For a short overview, see e.g., Ulrich Brasche, *Europäische Integration*, 4th ed. (Berlin: De Gruyter, 2017).

of the discredited category of the nation (at least for the moment) in favour of a more inclusive history. How attractive this was can be demonstrated in a short anecdote. When a group of German historians met in Göttingen in 1946, Peter Rassow allegedly coined the slogan: "Leave German history behind, onwards to European history."[8]

There is an irony to this strategy: although today Europe is used as a post-national catchword, in the 1930s the fascist and national-socialist movements had drawn on the idea of a "new Europe." From 1943 at the latest, NS-propaganda tried to present Adolf Hitler as a heroic figure who would reunite the "European" empire of Charlemagne that had been sepa-rated by the ruler's grand-sons.[9] Thus, the successful intro-duction of Europe as a formula for a positive, democratic post-war organization was by no means obvious. In hindsight, certain parallels between the fascist and the (later) demo-cratic constructions of a concept of Europe are astonishing—one case in point being the "Karlspreis" itself that had an explicitly anti-Bolshevistic orientation at the outset.

As to research by medievalists, works on the history of the notion and idea of Europe were motivated by contem-porary needs and interests—a phenomenon that was made explicit in an 1980 article in which Denys Hay reflected on his 1957 monograph *Europe—The Emergence of an Idea*.[10]

---

**8** See Winfried Schulze, *Deutsche Geschichtswissenschaft nach 1945* (Munich: Oldenbourg, 1989), 160: "Fort aus der deutschen und hinein in die europäische Geschichte."

**9** Oschema, "Ein Karl für alle Fälle," 55–56; Vanessa Conze, *Das Europa der Deutschen. Ideen von Europa in Deutschland zwischen Reich-stradition und Westorientierung (1920-1970)* (Munich: Oldenbourg, 2005), 61–62.

**10** Denys Hay, "Europe Revisited: 1979," *History of European Ideas* 1 (1980): 1–6 at 3: "To say that historians are victims, or at any rate mirrors, of their own time is not to say very much. But some of us who were writing about the European idea were, I suspect, doing more than that. We were not only assuming a kind of historical inevitability in the notion but trying positively to encourage the process. There was a Hegelian 'spirit of Europe' and we either

Together with Jürgen Fischer's dissertation on *Oriens—Occidens—Europa* and a small number of other publications, Hay's study nonetheless provided an important and enduring basis for future research: whereas many authors preferred to focus on the cultural features of medieval societies in "Europe," Hay and Fischer scrutinized the concept connected to the name. In both cases the results were less inspiring than they had hoped for, and after careful analysis they were forced to conclude that there were no "roots" of a political concept of Europe in the Middle Ages. Obviously, medieval authors used the name of the continent, but they did not choose to hang more elaborate political ideas on it.

This conclusion dominated the mainstream of historical research for decades: Between the 1960s and 1980s a certain number of studies revisited the subject without making any fundamental dents to the established picture. As the following chapters will show, this picture relied on two important factors that determined the results: On the one hand, the historians of the 1940s and 1950s were looking for an explicitly "political" idea of Europe. Due to the difficulties identifying a specifically "political" discourse in the medieval material, especially before the thirteenth century and the reception of Aristotelian works and ideas, this focus was bound to produce limited results. On the other hand, these authors tended to work on sources that were considered central and relevant. While these sources might include certain theological texts, such as St. Augustine's works, they mainly comprised historiographical texts—that is, chronicles and annals—as well as charters. These factors led to the production of a limited picture, one that needs to be modified, since modern research more willingly includes texts beyond the earlier mainstream and many texts have become more easily available in recent editions and through databases that provide access to large collections. A more open approach to our question, one that is not limited to strictly political uses of the notion of Europe,

---

analyzed its elements or blew wind into its sails, but we did not question that in the end it would prevail."

in tandem with the inclusion of larger corpora of texts (and images as well as material artefacts), helps us to develop a more adequate picture.

## Western Exclusivity or Integration of the East? How Medievalists Change Perspectives

Despite all possible criticism, the contributions of Hay, Fischer, and others provided important probes and early syntheses: while medievalists continued to reflect on the medieval notion of Europe in the 1970s and 1980s, by and large they did not develop fundamentally new approaches or work on hitherto unknown material. Anna-Dorothee von den Brincken's instructive article on Europe in medieval cartography, published in 1973, should be mentioned as one of the few notable exceptions to this rule.[11] Most authors were, however, content to synthesize the existing material and positions, thereby providing little more than useful and erudite overviews on the subject.[12] In addition, the sustained importance of some older works, including Gollwitzer's habilitation thesis or Hay's book, was evidenced by the release of new editions in the 1960s.

A conveniently available and well-informed synthesis of this older research-tradition was provided by Rudolf Hiestand in his 1991 article, "'Europa' im Mittelalter": according to him, an explicit "idea of Europe" was virtually absent from medieval thinking and in fact "replaced" the Middle Ages, since it characterized early modern thinking. While the notion remained marginal for most of the period, moments of more intensive use could be witnessed at the Carolingian courts of the ninth century as well as in certain moments when Latin

---

**11** Anna Dorothee von den Brincken, "Europa in der Kartographie des Mittelalters," *Archiv für Kulturgeschichte* 55 (1973): 289–304.

**12** Ralf-Joachim Sattler, *Europa. Geschichte und Aktualität des Begriffes* (Braunschweig: Limbach, 1971); Manfred Fuhrmann, *Europa— Zur Geschichte einer kulturellen und politischen Idee* (Constance: Universitätsverlag, 1981); see, however, Fuhrmann, *Alexander von Roes*.

Christianity felt threatened from the outside, for instance during the Mongol and the Ottoman expansions (thirteenth and fifteenth century respectively). The latter of these developments coincided with a new humanist tradition that finally led to the creation of a genuinely political concept of Europe, one that was first characterized by its strong religious overtones: Pope Pius II, the humanist Enea Silvio Piccolomini, was generally identified as the (re-)inventor of the collective noun "Europeans," and his texts repeatedly styled the conflict between Christians and the Muslim Ottomans as a confrontation between Asia and Europe.

The Europe of late twentieth-century medievalists focused by and large on the western and central parts of the continent that were dominated by Catholic Latin Christianity. Debates mostly revolved around questions that concerned, for example, the role of the Carolingian Empire in the creation of this "historical Europe": while Dawson identified it as the decisive core, Geoffrey Barraclough and others underlined the constitutive effects of the empire's dissolution and the developments of the eleventh and twelfth centuries.[13] Nevertheless, most medievalists were happy to accept a definition that excluded the eastern Christian world, especially Byzantium.

This juxtaposition between a "real Europe" in the West and its specific, constitutive antipode in the East placed Byzantium as a part of the "Orient." This notion coincided neatly with Western medievalists' own political environment (dominated in Europe by the "Iron Curtain"), which sustained a profound upheaval in 1989/90. In the aftermath of the fall of the Berlin Wall and the resulting reorganization of political structures in Europe and beyond, the question of what "Europe" was supposed to mean was once again on the table. After 1990 the situation became as intellectually pressing as ever it had been after 1945. It is thus hardly surprising that

---

**13** Geoffrey Barraclough, *The Crucible of Europe. The 9th and 10th Centuries in European History* (London: Thames Hudson, 1976), 8–11; cf. already Joseph Calmette, *L'effondrement d'un empire et la naissance d'une Europe, IXe–Xe siècles* (Paris: Aubier, 1941).

questions about Europe, its identity, and its history, were once again widely debated—and that medievalists (again) sought to contribute to the discussion (*BE* 66-74). Some studies that appeared immediately after 1990 continued to follow the paths that had been established decades earlier: Dieter Mertens, for example, published an excellent article ("Europäischer Friede und Türkenkrieg im Spätmittelalter") on the notion of Europe in the context of the wars against the "Turks" in 1991, and a special issue of *Past & Present* presented a series of articles on Europe in history, including a contribution by Karl Leyser on the Carolingians' use of the term.[14] Several publications by historians referred explicitly to the events of 1989/90 in order to justify their choice of subject,[15] while others did their best to warn of the problems that might arise from an eagerness to use historical material to answer contemporary questions.[16]

One of the most interesting effects, however, was a rapid reorientation of interpretations: In fact, the numerous publications that appeared in quick succession only rarely sought to present hitherto undiscussed source material. Still, many authors accepted that Europe had always included the eastern parts of the continent as well, an idea which contradicted the view that medievalists had generally held for several decades. A stunning example of this was furnished by an exhibition (and the accompanying publication) on "Europe's Centre around 1000" that identified the regions of Poland, Bohemia, Hungary, and Bavaria as the centre of the continent. The project was organized under the auspices of the Council of Europe and shed light on regions that were hitherto largely neglected by Western medievalists. However, the conceptual question of what "Europe" was supposed to

---

14 *Past & Present* 137 (1992); see Leyser, "Concepts of Europe".

15 See *The Idea of Europe*, cited above, with a strong focus on modern developments, from the eighteenth century onwards.

16 Peter Segl, "Europas Grundlegung im Mittelalter," in *Europa— aber was ist es? Aspekte seiner Identität in interdisziplinärer Sicht*, ed. Jörg A. Schlumberger and Peter Segl (Cologne: Böhlau, 1994), 21-43.

mean in this context was barely discussed. From a critical perspective, one might conclude that the process of Europeanization as presented in the catalogue mainly consisted in the successful integration of the Eastern regions into the cultural sphere of the "Occident."[17]

The result has been that it is less clear than ever what "Europe" should mean for medievalists, be it in cultural terms or in a geographical sense. While some still adhere to the "Carolingian model," others include the Greek and Slavic Eastern parts of the continent without necessarily making clear where an eastern border lies. In addition, the southern border, mostly identified with the Mediterranean, might also be called into question when one accepts the latter's role as a region of cultural contact rather than as a border between two landmasses and their inhabitants. All in all, the debates in the decades around the year 2000 have produced neither a consensus nor a clear opposition of valid models and approaches. Instead, these debates appear to have been quietly laid to rest by the development of new perspectives discussed under the label of "Mediterranean Studies" or the "Global Middle Ages"—both of which put a greater emphasis on transcultural perspectives.[18]

To adequately understand this state of affairs, it must be underscored that divergences often concern publications and reflections about the "reality" or an allegedly "true nature" of Europe. Turning now to the history of the notion itself and its accompanying ideas might provide some helpful insight and clarify what premodern authors understood by Europe when they used the word.

---

**17** See the catalogue *Europas Mitte um 1000. Beiträge zur Geschichte, Kunst und Archäologie*, ed. Alfried Wieczorek and Hans-Martin Hinz, 3 vols. (Darmstadt: Wissenschaftliche Buchgesellschaft, 2000).

**18** See the series "Mediterranean Studies," published by the Centre for Mediterranean Studies at the Ruhr-University Bochum. For the influence of the "global turn," see Thomas Ertl and Klaus Oschema, "Les études médiévales après le tournant global," *Annales. Histoire, Sciences Sociales* 74, no. 4 (2021): 787–801.

Chapter 2

# Foundations in Antiquity

As is often the case with topics that pertain to a "history of ideas" of the Middle Ages, an analysis of the notion of Europe in this period is not possible without considering the foundations in Antiquity. In the case of Europe this begins with the word itself, whose origins are still not entirely clear. Some researchers propose a (reconstructed) Phoenician root *'rb*, related to the Hebrew *'ereb* and referring to the "evening." Others prefer a genuinely Greek etymology, based on *eurý-* (broad) or *eûros* (breadth), which coincides with interpretations by antique authors. Equally, a connection with *eurós* (mouldiness, decay) might be possible, though it seems rather unlikely.[1]

Medieval authors, who were often fascinated by the origins of words and their etymology which they took to represent "real" meaning, hardly ever commented on Europe from this perspective. They mostly limited their reflections to the more factual observation that Europe was the third part of the world and received its name from the princess *Europa*—a tradition that is already attested to in Roman sources: *Europam tertiam orbis partem ab Europa, Agenoris filia, certum est appellari* (Europe, the third part of the world, is certainly named after Europa, the daughter of Agenor: Sextus Pompeius Festus, second century CE; *BE* 83). Only a few medieval texts commented on the Greek origin, such as, for example,

---

1 Immanuel Musäus, "Der Name Europas," in *Europa—Stier und Sternenkranz*, 341–51.

one anonymous glossator who commented on Orosius's work and explained, at some point between the seventh and the ninth century CE: *Eurupa grece tellus* (Europe means "land" in Greek) (*BE* 84). It is only at the beginning of the fourteenth century that we find more elaborate etymological explanations: Referring to the combination of *eu* and *ripa*, for example, the author of an *Ovide moralisé* stated that "Europe means good shore," and Bernhard of Kremsmünster proposed an analogous explanation at roughly the same time (*BE* 85).

## A Tripartite World— The Greeks Invent the Continents

Although the origins of the name of Europe refer to a (mythological) person, it seems helpful to begin with a short outline of the image of the world in ancient Greek geography.[2] While there might have been older forerunners, the earliest extant author who distinguished between two landmasses (or "continents" in modern terminology)—that is, Europe and Asia—was Hekataios of Milet around 500 BCE. Hekataios also proposed to modify this image, established prior to him, by adding a third part of the world, Libya (Africa)—an idea that was highly debated for some time. When Herodotus discussed the earth's structure in the fifth century BCE, he ridiculed any attempt to distinguish between different landmasses before finally accepting the tripartite structure. The originality of this model cannot be stressed enough: in a world where no aerial photos were available, let alone satellite images, the more obvious ways to structure the world would have been in accordance with the cardinal directions of sunrise and sunset, perhaps supplemented by a perpendicular axis. Choosing a tripartite structure, instead of a bipartite or quadripartite one, was thus an expression of extraordinary observation and reflection.

In cultural terms, however, Herodotus stressed the antagonism between the Greeks and the Persians, which could be

---

**2** On "Europe" in Greek Antiquity, see Danielle Jouanna, *L'Europe est née en Grèce* (Paris: L'Harmattan, 2009).

translated into a confrontation between Europe and Asia (see chap. 3 below). Over the following centuries, the debates about the structure of the landmasses that form the *ecumene*, the inhabitable earth, lingered on. Most authors came down on the side of the tripartite description, but Varro or Seneca still preferred the bipartite model.[3] In fact, both models could even be combined, as is attested to in St. Augustine's *De civitate Dei* or *The City of God* (bk. 16, chap. 17): in the late fourth century CE, this Church Father explained that the earth could be divided into two halves and that Asia occupied one of them (namely, the east), while Europe and Africa shared the other (the west). But as this description already makes clear, the formula of a world that consisted of three "parts" (the geographical notion "continent" is a modern invention, and I will only use it for sake of convenience)[4] became the standard model inherited by medieval authors. In addition, the *ecumene* was supposed to occupy only one quarter segment of a spheric globe—while there are a few texts that describe a flat Earth,[5] they remained quite rare. The overwhelming majority of medieval authors clearly understood the earth to be spherical in form.

## The Abduction of a Princess— Europe and the Violent God

Apart from the underlying geographical ideas, the question of the names of the "continents" played an important role. While the name of Africa was readily explained with pseudo-etymological reasonings by later authors, all the parts of the world

---

**3** Mauntel et al., "Mapping Continents," 300–304.

**4** Martin Lewis and Kären Wigen, *The Myth of Continents. A Critique of Metageography* (Berkeley: University of California Press, 1997) is fundamental; see also Christian Grataloup, *L'invention des continents. Comment l'Europe a découpé le monde* (Paris: Larousse, 2009).

**5** Andrew H. Merrills, *History and Geography in Late Antiquity* (Cambridge: Cambridge University Press, 2005); Schleicher, *Cosmographia Christiana*.

and their names became connected with mythological stories early on. The name of "Europa" is first attested in a poem by Hesiod (ca. 700 BCE), who mentioned her as one of the three thousand Oceanids (the daughters of Oceanus and Thetys). Homer, who might have lived at roughly the same time, did not mention Europa explicitly in his *Ilias*, but he referred to the daughter of "famous Phenix" who "gave birth to the god-like sons Minos and Rhadamanthys" (*BE* 85–86). This short allusion already attests to some of the elements that came to constitute the core of many poetic renderings of the myth of Europa. In its most elaborate form, this myth is known through a poem by Moschos (second century BCE), who related the famous story of Europa's abduction by Zeus/Jupiter in the form of a bull: the daughter of King Agenor of Tyrus played on the beach when the tauriform god appeared, abducted her, and transported her over the sea to Crete, where she gave birth to several sons (Minos, Rhadamanthys, Sarpedon).

Several versions of this myth exist that might also be used to explain the development of cultural traits and features. Most ancient sources tended to focus on those mythological aspects, which they frequently enriched with bucolic elements. Although the religious dimension remains quite vague, at some places, like Gortyn in Crete, a cult—mentioned by Pliny the Elder in his *Natural History* (bk. 12, chap. 5, §11)—seems to have developed. It is particularly noteworthy that ancient Greek and Roman authors had already begun to furnish rationalized explanations for the events depicted in the myth: Herodotus, for example, held that Europa was simply abducted by a Cretan ship.

While the myth of Princess Europa clearly dominates in our sources, some texts also mention a King Europs as the name-giver of the continent. One of these relatively rare textual examples is found in Justinus's *Epitome*; in the fourth century, St. Jerome, another Church Father, identified this Europs as ruling over the northwestern part of the world at the time of Abraham and Ninus. Later, Europs appeared in St. Augustine's *De civitate Dei* and in Gregory of Tours' *Ten Books of Histories* as the ruler of the Sicyonians, but neither author related him explicitly to the name of the continent. A number of medieval authors continued to refer to him, though infrequently, and he appears in works by Frechulf of Lisieux, Otto of Freising, Rudolf of Ems, as well as in Gossouin of Metz's *Image du monde* (mid-thirteenth century). Gossouin explicitly identified Europs as the name-giver of the continent, but this remained exceptional: in most cases, Europs was only mentioned in passing and it was Europa who dominated the scene.[6]

## Europe versus Asia? Cultural and Political Ideas

Another important aspect of discussions about "Europe" concerns the cultural and political ideas that became attached to the name, especially in the confrontation with Asia. While some modern authors saw this constellation as quite important, others warned of modern distortions leading to overestimating its role in Antiquity. The difficulties for an adequate understanding are even underlined by the observation that it is not always clear what ancient authors meant when they spoke of Europe: they were mostly familiar with the regions adjoining the Mediterranean, and their ideas about the regions which were farther inland remained vague.

When Herodotus emphasized the confrontation between the two parts of the world (i.e., Europe and Asia), he tended to also underscore the role played by the Hellespont that separated Greeks and Persians (he considered himself a Greek, even though he came from Halikarnassos in Asia Minor). Like Aischylos, and in a way that was unknown to the *Ilias*, Herodotus interpreted the Hellespont as a meaningful border and part of the divinely ordained order of the world; crossing it in the attempt to extend one's rule beyond this line was an act of hubris that defied the Gods. However, the main protagonists in Herodotus's *History* remained the Greek and the Persians themselves—and while they might have represented Europe and Asia implicitly, they were not explicitly identified as such.

---

**6** For the material on Europs, see Oschema, *Bilder von Europa*, 104, 165, and 204–6.

All in all, the confrontation between Europe and Asia seems to have remained a mostly literary motif that was seldom invoked in manifestly political contexts. Certainly, one famous exception to this was Isokrates who advocated an alliance between Hellenes and Macedonians under the overarching category of Europe in the fourth century BCE. In order to do so, he also drew on ideas about the connection between the environment and the regional character of populations. This was based on the theory that the hemispheres of the earth were separated into different climates (most authors count seven that extended from the extremely hot climate at the equator to the extremely cold at the polar regions); a pseudo-Hippocratic text on *Airs, Waters, Places* had concluded that Asians were unfit for war and were naturally servile, while Europeans were superior on the battlefield and in terms of culture and politics. This text did not vilify Asia, though; the author presents it as a region of mild climate, fertility, and cultivated habits, but also considers these characteristics not conducive to produce the courage and bravery that supposedly characterized Europeans (*BE* 92–93).

This specific "climate theory" continued to influence thinkers well into the Middle Ages and the modern period, but it remained flexible and could lead to different interpretations: Aristotle used it in his *Politics* as did Plato in his *State* (*BE* 92). In contrast to earlier interpretations, they underlined the virtue of balance: the Greeks thus became the people who inhabited the most proficient regions, since they lived on the border between Europe and Asia and could thus profit from the advantages of both.

From a more general perspective, Greek authors rarely explicitly praised Europe—unlike their later Roman colleagues, who sometimes established a sort of natural hierarchy amongst the continents: Strabo, for instance, emphasized the geographical advantages of Europe which "produced virtuous people and good political systems"; for Pliny the Elder, Europe was simply the most beautiful of the continents (*BE* 93).

Despite these (all in all quite rare) valorizing comments, a genuinely political dimension of Europe seems, if not entirely absent, at least secondary. Roman perceptions of rulership soon developed a universal outlook, and with the growth of the Roman Empire around the Mediterranean the division between the landmasses became secondary. Only rarely was the idea of universal rule formulated on the basis of domination over the continents: a bas-relief from the first century BCE that celebrated Alexander the Great's position dominating Europe and Asia was unique (and furnishes the oldest known personification of the continents, in contrast to depictions of the mythological figures).[7] Equally exceptional is an inscription dated 7 CE that was found on the island of Philae in the Nile which praises Augustus as "Lord over Europe and Asia" (*BE* 94–95).

The medieval world thus inherited a small set of ideas that were connected to the notion of Europe. First, the name that referred to one of the three parts of the known and inhabitable *ecumene*. Second, the connection to Europa, a Phoenician or Tyrian princess who was abducted by Zeus/Jupiter in the form of a bull and transported to Crete, where she gave birth to several sons. And third, the use ancient authors from Greece and Rome made of the terminology and the structure of the parts of the world in politically or culturally charged contexts. These latter instances remained exceptional, however, and were never strictly formalized.

---

**7** See Oschema, *Bilder von Europa*, 94 and fig. 3.

Chapter 3

# Moments of Transformation—
# Europe in the Early Middle Ages

The ancient heritage that I sketched in the previous chapter
became part and parcel of the later medieval traditions. A
series of key authors, including St. Augustine, Orosius, Cassiodorus, and most importantly Isidore of Seville with his *Etymologies,* transmitted central aspects of this knowledge to
the post-Roman world. At the same time, the slow assertion
of Christianity inevitably led to significant changes in atti-
tude towards the individual aspects that the notion of Europe
evoked. While the geographical element was quite unprob-
lematic—in fact, it fitted into the intellectual framework of a
religion whose God had a tripartite nature—the mythological
motifs were quite different. This chapter will first present how
early Christian authors reacted to the myth of Europa, before
turning to their treatment of aspects of geographical structure and administrative order. It will conclude with a brief presentation of the surprising increase of references to Europe
in a religious context.

## Against Paganism: Christian Reactions
## to the Myth of "Europa"

The important Christian thinkers of the fourth and fifth centuries were well-versed in canonical knowledge of the ancient
world. St. Augustine received an excellent education in the

sense of classical *paideia*[1] and the same holds true for others, who also did their best to collect and transmit the canon of knowledge. Cassiodorus, who founded the monastery of Vivarium towards the mid-sixth century, organized much of this canon in his *Institutiones*, and Isidore of Seville's *Etymologies* assembled a wealth of information in quasi-encyclopaedic form in the early seventh century.

Well acquainted as they were with the traditions in "pagan" texts, we can observe how Christian authors reacted to the myths and stories they encountered. In the case of Europa, two separate strategies can be identified: On the one hand, several authors tried to rationalize the story of the abduction (as did Herodotus). Lactantius (d. ca. 320), for example, interpreted the "bull" as imagery on the sail (a *tutela*) of the abductors' boat (*BE* 101). Most Christian authors, on the other hand, used the story of Europa's abduction to demonstrate the moral inferiority of the pagan gods. From this perspective, Europa's fate could either be discussed separately or in passages that collected several examples of Zeus/Jupiter's adulterous activities. Isidore of Seville, for instance, described Jupiter as "incestuous" and "adulterous" (*Etymologies*, bk. 8, chap. 9, §§34–36). He illustrated this verdict by referring to the god's famous transformations into different animals, which allowed him to seduce innocent girls and boys.

As Jürgen Fischer has already pointed out, due to competition between the different traditions, Christian reactions towards the pagan myths tended at first to be quite aggressive, but they soon became relatively "neutralized." St. Augustine still qualified the pagan myths as "vain fables," but his treatment of them lacked the fierce judgement of earlier texts. This did not exclude more polemical positions, which can be found in Dracontius's *Romulea* (ca. 490) or much later, around 1500, in the works of humanists (*BE* 104). The overall impression is that this once "religious" matter soon became the material of a "cultural" tradition. This included references

---

I  Peter Brown, *Augustine of Hippo: A Biography*, rev. ed. (Berkeley: University of California Press, 2000).

to diverse phenomena, such as the naming of the constellation of *Taurus*, which Isidore saw in immediate relation to the story of Europa. His polemics remained quite subtle in this case: though the constellation was named *Taurus* (bull), he described the god's transformation into an ox (*bos*), and thereby symbolically evoked the idea of a more harmless, castrated animal (also a possible allusion to the symbol for St. Luke the Evangelist) (*Etymologies*, bk. 3, chap. 71, §24).

## Integrating Pagan Knowledge: Concepts of Geographical and Administrative Order

Many elements of ancient tradition became part of the Latin Christian canon in the form of "neutralized" cultural knowledge. In our case, this was primarily true for the naming of the landmass that occupied the northwestern quarter of the known *ecumene*: Europe was frequently described as the "third part of the world" (*tertium pars mundi*). The importance of this seemingly simple formula can hardly be overstated, since its identification was not clear from the outset: From the perspective of Roman imperial administration, the name could also designate a province between Lydia and Thracia in the eastern part of the empire. That early Christian authors knew about this more restricted interpretation is attested by a list of provinces mentioned by Hilarius of Poitiers in the mid-fourth century and a series of other texts, mostly administrative in character.

While this more limited interpretation continued to be used for several centuries, most authors seem to have understood Europe in the larger geographical sense of the *pars mundi*. In addition, the earlier uncertainties about the continent's borders gradually disappeared. Practically all authors agreed that the continents were separated by bodies of water, but there seems to have been quite a lively debate amongst Greek and Roman thinkers concerning their actual identification. Although nearly everyone agreed that the Mediterranean separated Europe from Africa, the borders between these two and Asia posed a much trickier problem.

The Nile soon became a consensual choice for the separation of Africa from Asia, but the Eastern border of Europe continued to be debated: ancient authors proposed either the Don or the Phasis (Rioni) in modern Georgia, but the latter slowly disappeared in medieval texts. Isidore and Bede, to name two important authors, spoke only of the Don. In the early eighth century the anonymous "Cosmographer of Ravenna" mentioned both options but, after a brief discussion, decided against the Phasis. In the centuries that followed, the Don, which was supposed to connect the Black Sea with the surrounding ocean in the north, prevailed (*BE* 109–11).

While the geographical basis of the tripartite world order was thus increasingly clarified (or rather simplified), the notion of Europe could also be used in contexts that concerned real administrative questions. The Roman provincial order continued to surface in the sources, making it sometimes difficult to decide what Europe referred to in specific cases. In addition, a small number of authors also attest to the possibility that one could conceptualize the separation of spheres of influence amongst Roman emperors and caesars by referring to the continental order: hence Theodoret of Kyros mentioned in the mid-fifth century that Valentinian had transferred the rule over Asia and Africa (or rather Egypt) to Valens, while he had kept Europe and the entire Occident for himself (*BE* 106–7). Several decades later, Cassiodorus also referred to Valentinian's rule over Europe. Even if the number of analogous examples remains narrow, they clearly demonstrate that the use of the continental order was not limited to strictly geographic contexts but could extend into the political and administrative sphere. Since both dimensions, the cosmographical and the administrative, could merge in these texts, it remains difficult to decide which one prevailed in the respective texts.

## Christianizing Europe: From St. Martin of Tours to Charlemagne

The most surprising development in this period concerned Christian authors' use of the name "Europe" in explicitly religious contexts. After all, the biblical texts rarely refer to the continents—some verses mention Asia (Acts 2:9, 6:9, etc.; 2 Cor. 1:8) and (more rarely) Africa (or rather *Libya*: Daniel 11:43), Europe does not appear at all—and the very outlook of Christianity had quickly become universal.

Nevertheless, individual Christian authors began to use the continent's name in religious contexts quite early, especially in hagiographic sources. This is particularly remarkable, as the cardinal directions of the north and the west (where Europe was situated) usually carried negative connotations and were even associated with demonic presence and activities. Earthly paradise and the coming of salvation, on the other hand, were identified with the east (and the sunrise). Seen from a strictly systematic perspective, there was simply no reason to talk about the continents at all.

It is thus surprising to see the relatively early development of a tradition that built upon older Jewish texts: According to the *Book of Jubilees* (*Sepher hayYobhelim*, ca. 160/150 BCE), Noah distributed the lands of the earth amongst his sons Shem, Ham, and Japeth by drawing lots.[2] The text, which relies on Genesis books 9–10, implies that Shem and his descendants received all of Asia; Ham—Africa; and Japeth—Europe, though the names of the continents are not used. Two centuries later, Flavius Josephus, who wrote his *History of the Jews* in Greek, reiterated this motif, once again without referring to the established borders between the continents. In the Christian tradition that followed, the idea that the descendants of Noah peopled the earth and divided the parts of the world between them according to this principle was further transmitted—first by Greek authors, like Epiphanius of Salamis in the late fourth century, and later also in Latin texts.

---

**2** For the material in this and in the following paragraph, see Oschema, *Bilder von Europa*, 113–17.

At the outset, authors such as St. Jerome did not seamlessly identify the Noachids' lands with the continents. In his *Commentary on Genesis*, Jerome made clear that each of the brothers also received a part of Asia. Later authors simplified this image: Eucherius of Lyon, writing in the late fifth century, plainly stated that Shem and his descendants received "Asia or the Orient," Ham "Africa or the South (*Meridiem*)," and Japheth "Europe or the Occident," thereby combining the structure of the continents with the order of the cardinal directions. In the following centuries, this identification between the sons of Noah and the continents became a well-established motif of Christian thinking. Simple texts like the *Joca monachorum* (sixth century) repeated the idea, as did more ambitious authors like the Venerable Bede, whose works contained a more precise as well as a simplified version.

Towards the early Middle Ages, Europe thus became "Japheth's share" (*portio Japhet*), as it is explicitly called in the work of the "Cosmographer of Ravenna" (eighth century) or in Alcuin's letters (ca. 800) (*BE* 116). This exegetical tradition should not be underestimated, since it furnished an effective basis for charging the continents further with cultural ideas: The tale of Noah and his sons in Gen. 9–10 not only provided a table of the people of the Earth, who were all believed to be descendants of Noah, but also established a clear hierarchy among them. According to Gen. 9, Noah got drunk on the first wine after the flood and denuded himself in his sleep. Ham saw his uncovered father and called his brothers to ridicule him. When Noah came to and realized what had happened, he blessed Shem and cursed Ham, while Japheth was prophesized to "dwell in the tents of Shem." Later interpretations identified Japheth as the forefather of the Christians, thereby providing an important first building block for more far-reaching interpretations of Europe as the continent where Christians lived—but this did not come more prominently to the fore before the twelfth century (see chap. 5 below).

Late Antiquity and the early Middle Ages witnessed further developments. On a relatively secular level, a number of authors referred to the borders of Europe as delimitations of a region under external threat.[3] The military campaigns by Attila the Hun were described in this way, for instance by Marcellinus Comes (ca. 520), whose narrative was further elaborated by Bede in his *Ecclesiastical History*. Even earlier, around ca. 400, Claudius Claudianus used the image of a Europe threatened by "barbarians," and Jordanes (ca. 550) presented the Goths as intruders who found their way from Scandinavia *in terram Europae* (into the land of Europe).

While some of these texts clearly tried to convey a sense of external menace, others, like Jordanes, described the migrations rather matter-of-factly. It is only in connection with further theological works that a potential change in the notion becomes plausible. In his *Commentary on the Apocalypse*, Apringius of Béja (mid-sixth century) identified the lands of Gog and Magog with Scythia, at the northeastern borders of Europe—thereby implying that peoples who came into Europe from these regions might be connected to the coming of the end-time. Other traditions that developed, lacked these negative features: In the texts about the origins of peoples, the *origo gentis*-narrations, Troy soon came to play a central role and the Franks were identified as descendants of a certain Francio, who came to settle in Europe after having destroyed parts of Asia (*BE* 122).

Quite a number of these narrations were clearly built on older traditions from Greco-Roman Antiquity or from Jewish texts. Others, however, confront us with new uses, hitherto unattested, all the while demonstrating an effort to include the once mainly secular entity that was "Europe" in a religious perspective on the world. A particularly surprising example is furnished by Sulpicius Severus (d. 420/425) in his *Dialogues*. Reflecting on the life of St. Martin of Tours, the author establishes a hierarchy of holiness amongst the three parts of the world. He admits that Asia and Egypt had produced large numbers of saints, only to conclude that the

---

**3** For the material in this and the following paragraph, see Oschema, *Bilder von Europa*, 119–24.

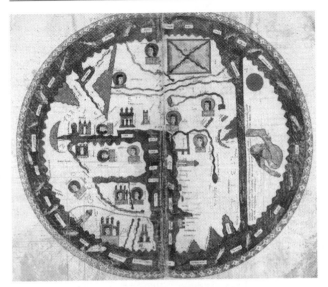

Fig. 1: World-map after Beatus of Liébana,
so-called "Osma-Beatus," 1086. Burgo de Osma,
Archivio de la Catedral, MS 1, fols. 34v–35r.
Public domain (Wikipedia).

extent of St. Martin's holiness alone sufficed to put Europe on
an equal rank (Dialogue 2 (3), chap. 17, §§ 6–7). While Venantius Fortunatus (d. 610) in his *Life of St. Martin* only referred
to the continents to explain that St. Paul had been active in
all of them, Sulpicius had already gone one important step
further: he not only described the propagation of Christianity
in a geographical framework that included all the parts of the
inhabited world, he also directly linked the parts of the world
to a discourse about religious value and sainthood.

In later centuries, analogous efforts can be seen in different media: The world-map (*mappamundi*) in a manuscript of
Beatus of Liébana's *Commentary on the Apocalypse* that is today
kept at Burgo de Osma, is one outstanding example (Fig. 1).

Beyond more basic geographical features, such as coast-lines, rivers, islands, and similar, the most striking element depicted on this map are the locations of the apostles' tombs. While five of them are situated in Asia and only one in Africa, Europe alone appears densely populated with six apostles and is thus visibly set apart.

At the time of Sulpicius Severus, such elaborate strategies to valorize Europe were not yet common, and they seem to have taken centuries to develop. The astonishing thing is that they developed at all! And although Sulpicius did not yet find immediate followers, Europe slowly and gradually became integrated in texts of religious character: early authors, like Paulinus of Nola (d. 431) or Dracontius (d. ca. 505), illustrated the universal vocation of Christianity in short passages that described how the apostles brought the religion from its places of origin in the Holy Land and in Egypt (i.e., in Asia and Africa) to Europe (*BE* 125).

In the case of St. Martin, Sulpicius's text did not find follow-ers, and later authors instead praised the saint's role for the entire world (*orbis*). In other cases, however, we can see the slow emergence of the idea that Europe constituted a reason-able framework for the diffusion of a saint's reputation. Writ-ing around 700, Aldhelm of Malmesbury underlined that Pope Silvester's miraculous workings covered "all the provinces of Europe" (*omnes Europae provincias*) and he also mentioned that the fame of Sts. Eustochia and Demetria "spread throughout Europe" (*per Europam diffunditur*) (*BE* 127).

Aldhelm's example is also revealing in another sense. It seems, in fact, that this kind of reference to Europe developed particularly early in the British Isles, especially Ireland: The anonymous author of the *Vita prima Samsonis*, written some time between the seventh and the ninth century, not only underlined that his protagonist's journey led him from Britain to Europe but also that the saint worked numerous miracles (with God's help, of course) "in Europe" (I.39; 46–47; 52–53).

Texts like these not only demonstrate that early medi-eval authors were familiar with the notion of Europe, but also that they could use it in contexts which transcended a purely "geographical" dimension. Societies and cultures that were used to interpret their world through the framework of religion, thereby investing potentially everything that surrounded them with symbolical value, would probably not have understood the concept of something "purely geographical."[4] In addition, the passages cited here imply that the authors did not merely think about the dissemination of specific information in a given space; instead they referred to Europe in order to demonstrate how widespread their protagonists' fame had become, thereby underlining the saint's importance. This practice implies that Europe had developed into a term that could be charged with meaning.

It must be said that the textual basis for this conclusion remains relatively modest. Nevertheless, the uses of the word by Sulpicius Severus or by the anonymous Irish authors of the following centuries should not simply be dismissed, for even if they appear quite exceptional, they provided a basis for later traditions, including the idea of a "Feast of all the saints of Europe" mentioned in the *Martyrology of Tallaght* in the mid-ninth century.[5]

---

**4** See Patrick Gautier Dalché, "Représentations géographiques de l'Europe—septentrionale, centrale et orientale—au Moyen Âge," in *Europa im Weltbild*, 63–79 at 63–64, and the contributions in *Geography and Religious Knowledge in the Premodern World*, ed. Christoph Mauntel (Berlin: De Gruyter, 2021).

**5** Oschema, "An Irish Making of Europe," 23.

Chapter 4

# Europe, Christianity, or Something Completely Different? Impressions from the Central Middle Ages

While it is not surprising that the notion of Europe became part of the vocabulary of medieval authors—after all, it was a central element of the geographical knowledge and the mythological lore they inherited from Greek and Roman Antiquity—the fact that it was used in contexts that transcended the ancient traditions is noticeable. Although early medieval sources rarely contain any kind of overtly "political" connotation, Europe was integrated into discourses that must be considered as religious, and it also served as an instrument to perceive, describe, and interpret the surrounding world.

Without becoming central for the description and analysis of societies and their organization, Europe continued to be used in a relatively broad range of situations, including contexts that come close to what modern readers might perceive to be political. A first apogee of this development is usually identified with the Carolingians between the mid-eighth and the early tenth centuries, and more specifically with the dominant figure of Charlemagne: modern authors after 1945 often repeated that he was called "Father of Europe" (*pater Europae*) by his contemporaries.[1] The first section of this chapter will demonstrate that this is not entirely false, but not wholly true either. Still, the use of the notion of Europe in the Carolingian period seems significant.

---

[1] Oschema, "Ein Karl für alle Fälle," 43–44 and 49.

## Nostalgic from the Outset— Remembering Charlemagne

Most modern historians of the medieval notion of Europe agree that the Carolingian period witnessed a first peak in the use of the term. The most prominent example certainly is the famous *Paderborn Epic*, which describes the encounter between Charlemagne and Pope Leo III at Paderborn in 799. Attacked and mutilated by his rivals in Rome, Leo fled to the king of the Franks to ask for his support, and Charlemagne's ensuing campaign to Italy culminated in his coronation as Roman emperor on Christmas 800. In the *Paderborn Epic*, the preceding events are described in detail and with lavish laudatory terms. The poet describes his king as "precious light" (*cara lux*—certainly a pun on Carolus) and refers to Europe in several instances. Charlemagne thus becomes the "lighthouse that illuminates Europe with his light" (*Europae quo celsa pharus cum luce coruscat*), the "venerable apex of Europe" (*Europae venerandus apex*) and finally, in the most famous phrase, the "Father of Europe" (*pater Europae*) (*BE* 138).

It is no surprise that this expression caught the eyes of modern medievalists when they were looking for the medieval roots of "Europe." But remarkable as it is, we should not ignore several details that remind us not to exaggerate its significance. First, the text praises both Charlemagne and his visitor, Pope Leo, in similarly acclamatory language—the latter being called the "pastor in the [entire] world" (*pastor in orbe*). As far as laudatory terms go, Leo thus seems even better off (though Charlemagne is also described as "head of the world," *caput orbis*, in the text). Second, we do not know exactly when the *Paderborn Epic* was composed and by whom. The author may have been Angilbert, the king's son-in-law, and it seems plausible that the poem was written shortly after Charlemagne's imperial coronation. Still, the designation as "Father of Europe" does not reflect the perspective of "the court poets": the poem is only known to us through one single, possibly incomplete surviving manuscript (today at the Zentralbibliothek at Zürich). Clearly, this was not a "bestseller," by any stretch of the imagination, even in terms of Carolingian poetry and its transmission. Finally, the very notion of a "Father of Europe" did not find any admirers who repeated it: the *Paderborn Epic* is the only known surviving medieval text that uses the phrase. Adémar of Chabannes, who wrote his *Chronicle* around 1030, seized on the imagery of the "father," but he fundamentally modified the framework: according to him, all the world, including the "pagans," bemoaned the demise of the great emperor in 814, whom he duly describes as "Father of the entire world" (*pater orbis*).[2]

A closer look at the evidence around 800 and its later reception thus leads to a quick and efficient deconstruction of the motif of the "European Charlemagne," which had been established so forcefully and efficiently after 1945. This does not mean, however, that older studies on the use of Europe in the Carolingian period were entirely wrong—they merely went overboard in their enthusiastic search for medieval forerunners: After all, the notion of Europe does not figure in any administrative or other writings emanating from the ruler's court itself, at least not in official contexts. Even Charlemagne's biographer Einhard, who wrote several years after his king's death, did not use it in his *Vita Karoli Magni*. All the evidence we have thus points towards a conclusion that Charlemagne did not perceive his empire or his rulership in European terms.

In many respects, this is not surprising. Since it did not designate an entity that was politically relevant, "Europe" simply didn't play any significant role in the diplomatic language of the early and Central Middle Ages. Only in a few cases does the name of the continent surface in texts of diplomatic character and letter exchanges. Around 600, Pope Gregory I ("the Great") wrote to Emperor Mauritius in Constantinople and complained of his neglect of the western parts of the empire. Consequently, Gregory explained, the "lands of Europe" (*in Europae partibus*) suffered a decline into barbarism and destruction (*BE* 123). This extraordinary picture, which was meant to incite the emperor to more

---

**2** Oschema, "Ein Karl für alle Fälle," 52.

action in the service of his empire, but also in service of the Church, is complemented by two equally exceptional letters from St. Columbanus to Gregory and to his successor Boniface IV (608–615). In both letters, Columbanus addressed the recipients with extraordinary formulas, praising Gregory as "the most revered Flower of all of parched Europe" and Boniface as "the most fair Head of all the Churches of Europe."[3] These formulas are as exceptional as they are enigmatic: did Columbanus, who did not shy away from conflicts, want to suggest that the popes' authority was effectively limited to Europe? And what was his motivation? We can only surmise that he wanted to imply a special role for the churches in his Irish home, who followed their own tradition in the calculation of Easter, but these interpretations remain hypothetical.

Over the course of the eighth century, Europe had still not become a particularly popular notion—neither in historiographical texts nor in any others, though the anonymous author of the so-called *Mozarabic Chronicle of 754* coined the term *Europenses* for the composite army of Charles Martel that confronted the troops of Abd ar-Rahman in 732 (or possibly 733) (*BE* 134). Unfortunately, we don't really know what the author from the Iberian Peninsula intended in his use of this collective name, for which only very few forerunners in ancient texts can be found. It is all too possible that he merely wanted to refer to soldiers from different regions beyond the Pyrenees. In any case, he did not find any followers in this usage and "Europeans" did not appear again until the late Middle Ages (see further in chap. 5 below).

At Charlemagne's court, "Europe" appeared most prominently in texts by authors of insular origin, that is Irish or British. The priest Cathwulf, for example, sent a letter in 775, in which he complimented the ruler on having been elevated to "the honour of the glory of the kingdom of Europe" (*regni*

---

**3** Klaus Oschema, "Columbanus and Europe," in *Making Europe: Columbanus and Identity in Early Medieval Europe*, ed. Conor Newman, Mark Stansbury, and Emmet Marron (Rennes: Presses universitaires de Rennes, 2022), 153–66 at 155.

*Europae*). Alcuin, whom the king had attracted to his court, underlined in letters to English addressees, that the Church in Europe (*in partibus Europae*) enjoyed peace (790) and he also used the name in a poem on St. Martin (*BE* 138–39).

A real increase in the use of the word can only be seen in the decades after the emperor's death (814).[4] In a number of panegyric poems from the ninth century, several poets referred to Europe to praise either the former ruler or their contemporary kings. In a poem addressed to Louis the Pious, Charlemagne's only surviving son, Theodulf of Orléans stated that God had given Louis the rule of the "realms of Europe" (*Europae regna*), adding that "the entire world" (*totus orbis*) bowed to the king's rule. The use of the plural is striking, when compared to the above-mentioned letter by Cathwulf, and might indicate the conscience of the Empire's disintegration. Only a few years later, Ardo Smaragdus wrote in his *Vita Benedicti*, that Louis, having become emperor, now presided over the "entire church of Europe" (*tocius ecclesia Europae*). For Sedulius Scottus, writing around 850, Charlemagne had been the "Lord of Europe"—but also the "resplendent Emperor of the entire world": *Caesar erat Karolus toto clarissimus orbe / Europae princeps, imperiale decus.*

While some of these passages evoke the idea of Europe as a meaningful unit, others clearly reflect the slow dissolution of what their authors perceived as having been an entity. Ermoldus Nigellus, who wrote shortly after Theodulf, for instance, equally spoke of the "realms of Europe" (*Europae regna*) and this idea of a plurality of kingdoms came to dominate the picture. While the later Carolingian poets repeatedly referred to Europe, their use of the term was characterized by very specific traits: On the one hand, they presented it as being under their ruler's authority and as being constituted by several units; on the other hand, they frequently made clear that the real vocation of emperorship resided in universal authority. Finally, their use of the notion of Europe had a

---

**4** For the material in the following three paragraphs, see Oschema, *Bilder von Europa*, 148–60.

nostalgic flavour: they were looking back to a more glorious past under Charlemagne and implicitly or explicitly deplored the loss of former greatness and unity.

This becomes more tangible under the sons of Louis the Pious, who formally separated their inheritance into several realms (first at Verdun in 843, then at Meerssen in 870), though they continued to underscore the bond between brothers. In the long run, it is thus hardly surprising that the nostalgic references to Europe became increasingly visible towards the end of the ninth and the beginning of the tenth century. One continuer of the *Annals of Fulda* spoke of "Europe, i.e., the realm of Charles" in his description of the events that followed the demise of Charles the Fat in 888. This great-grandson of Charlemagne had been the last Carolingian ruler who united, virtually by accident, all the Carolingian realms in his hand. After his death, the realm was divided into several kingdoms that became increasingly independent. The critical perspective of the *Annals'* anonymous author becomes all too clear when he comments that "many kinglets" (*multi reguli*) arose in Europe at that time. Charlemagne, on the other hand, represented a time of ancient glory when Europe had been united under the ruler's authority—at least, some authors imagined it this way. For Nithard (d. 845), the emperor left Europe filled with all his good (*omni bonitate*) when he died. And nearly a century later, Notker "the Stammerer," a monk at St. Gallen, repeatedly mentioned in his *Gesta Karoli* that all—or nearly all—of the nobility of Europe had been present at Charlemagne's court and feasts.

All of these passages remained relatively informal, however. They demonstrate that authors of this period had a certain idea of Europe and that the name of the continent could be used to praise the extent and importance of a ruler's authority, but almost no one connected it with the more formal concept of rulership in the sense of an official title. The only exceptions, once again, come from insular material. Looking back to the late Roman period, the *Historia Brittonum* (ca. 830) attributed the "rule over all of Europe" (*imperium... totius Europae*) to an Emperor Maximian. It can be a matter of debate whether or not *imperium* can be translated here to mean, in the more formal sense, a political unit or, more abstractly, "the command." Either way this formula may have provided a model for the writers of the *Chronicum Scotorum* or the *Annals of Ulster* when they called Charlemagne the "King of the Franks" (*rex Francorum*)—which he definitively was—and the "Emperor of all of Europe" (*totius Europe imperator*)[5]—which he neither was nor claimed to be. Since Sedulius Scotus was also of insular origin (as were Cathwulf and Alcuin), the most outspoken texts that connected Charlemagne with Europe thus came from authors who had either migrated from England or Ireland to the continent, or who described the events from their insular perspective.

This does not mean that the widespread notion of the Carolingian period as a first apogee in the history of the notion of Europe is entirely erroneous. The word seems indeed to have been used more frequently from the late-eighth century onwards. Carolingian annals, for example, repeatedly mention events that they thought concerned all of Europe, including a bovine disease that spread "all over Europe" in 810. While these rather inconspicuous references attest to the presence of the word, they are quite far from the seemingly triumphant overtones of the *pater Europae*. This extraordinary expression remained singular in its own time and beyond. And when Europe was referred to in the Carolingian panegyrics and historiography, it mostly conveyed the idea of a former unity that had ceased to exist. All in all, one is tempted to conclude that this Carolingian Europe had never been a reality, and that poets and historiographers tried to write it into existence.

## Shadows from Dark Times— Europe after the Carolingians

Despite this somewhat resigned observation, Europe did not disappear in the tenth century: although the Carolingian

---

5 Oschema, "An Irish Making of Europe," 20–21.

Empire gave way to a number of increasingly independent kingdoms, historiographers continued to refer to Europe. In many cases, it remains quite difficult, however, to understand what motivated them and what exactly they meant when they used the name. In reply to Karl Leyser's analysis of the Carolingian use of the term, Timothy Reuter drily commented that Europe mostly meant nothing more than "my back-yard and anywhere else that counts."[6]

While this might have often been the case, it remains noticeable how frequently we find the name in contexts where one might not necessarily expect it. During the ninth to eleventh centuries, pertinent passages appear in Irish annals: the *Annals of Loch Cé*, for example, qualify Brian Ború (d. 1014) as "Augustus of the Northwest of Europe" and proudly describe the erudite cleric Crocran (d. 1040) as the wisest in Europe.[7] This tendency to use the term has formerly been explained as an indication of the Irish clerics' knowledge of Greek. Although Walter Berschin has thrown reasonable doubt on the actual linguistic proficiency of the Irish,[8] this does not entirely invalidate the observation that they cultivated a predilection for Greek.

An analogous case might be the *Historia Romana*, written by Landulfus Sagax in late tenth-century Italy. The fact that he relied on sources with Greek origins, might explain his relatively prominent use of Europe. At the same time, it remains noteworthy that Landulfus chose to use the word even in contexts that were closer to his own time, for instance when he explained how the Muslims had come to Spain—which he explicitly situates in Europe—where they lived to his own day (*Europe Hispaniam habitarunt usque ad presens tempus*) (*BE*

---

6 Leyser, "Concepts of Europe"; Timothy Reuter, "Medieval Ideas of Europe and their Modern Historians," *History Workshop* 33 (1992): 176–80 at 178.

7 Oschema, "An Irish Making of Europe," 25.

8 Walter Berschin, "Griechisches bei den Iren," in *Die Iren und Europa im früheren Mittelalter*, ed. Heinz Löwe, 2 vols. (Stuttgart: Klett-Cotta, 1982), 1:501–10 at 510.

154). The name was thus part of Landulfus's active vocabu-lary. This is all the more significant, as Europe appears no less than twenty-one times in Frechulf of Lisieux's *Historiarum libri XII* (ca. 830), but almost exclusively in passages that treat the distant past: the distribution of lands amongst Noah's sons, the abduction of Europa, the migration of Francio from Troy to Europe, or the realm submitted to the rulership of Emper-ors Valentian and Gratian. Many of these passages rely on older sources, such as St. Jerome's *Chronicle* or Cassiodorus's *Historia ecclesiastica*. Frechulf willingly adopted the wording in these cases, but he did not use Europe to describe events that were closer to his own day.

Seen against this background, it remains noteworthy that texts from the Frankish realms in the tenth century contin-ued to use the term Europe from time to time. Perhaps they were inspired by the model of Carolingian panegyrics? In any case, Widukind of Corvey praised King Henry I as "Lord of the World and greatest of the kings of Europe" (*rerum dominus et regum maximus Europae*; from *Deeds of the Saxons*, bk. 1, chap. 41) and underlined that Henry's son Otto I had liberated "nearly all of Europe" from the Hungarians (bk. 1, chap. 19). Otto II, finally, had become so mighty that neither Germany, Italy, nor France—and not even all of Europe could contain his power (bk. 1, chap. 34). Such an acclamation still does not imply a more formal conception of Europe in the sense of formal rulership and actual titles, but the author's use of the word demonstrates that Europe had become a meaningful, albeit mostly virtual, category. Although it did not relate to any tangible realm, the word could serve to underline a rul-er's power and rank. Indeed, this openness and uncertainty is what made it suitable for the praise of the ruler.

Widukind was not the only author who used the word: according to the *Annals of Quedlinburg*, for example, Otto III was not only acclaimed by the people of Rome during his cor-onation in 996, but also by the people of "nearly all of Europe." At the court of Otto's successor, Emperor Henry II, the same text saw "all the noblemen of Europe" come together (as did Notker at the court of Charlemagne). If the anonymous author might simply have been following his Carolingian model in these cases, he also coined a quite singular image. Under the year 1022 he mentions how Henry II returned to his realm north of the Alps and was only accompanied by a small contingent of troops, except those that "mother Europe" (*mater Europa*) had accorded him. Once again, this formula invites speculation: according to Jürgen Fischer, Europe should be identified with "Germany" in this case, since all the troops that met with Henry in Pavia had come from north of the Alps.[9] While this interpretation cannot be entirely excluded, the text itself does not make it explicit.

Older studies, like Fischer's, frequently held that the notion of Europe was rarely used after the ninth century. In addition, the passages where it appeared allegedly showed a tendency to limit it to purely geographical terms. In contrast to this rather negative observation, the examples mentioned should suffice to show that the situation was quite different: even in the tenth and early eleventh centuries—that is, in a period for which only a relatively low number of written texts survive—we still find examples where Europe is used as a laudatory phrase. While some of these passages might depend on older models, our authors also used the term in ways that were not overly creative but nonetheless independent.

This observation and corrective is all the more important since a number of sources demonstrate how Europe could be used in administrative and even religious contexts. In 853, for example, Pope Leo IV explained in a letter to Ignatius, the patriarch of Constantinople, that he could not accept a pallium (an ecclesiastical vestment) that the latter had sent him: According to Leo, his own church of Rome, which he calls the "teacher and head of all churches," did not receive pallia, but rather sent them to other churches "all over Europe" (*BE* 158). This expression may seem merely geographic (which begs the question: what is meant by Europe in this specific context?)—but reducing it to geography alone overlooks the more important question: why would a pope, who

---

**9** Fischer, *Oriens—Occidens—Europa*, 107–12.

claimed universality, limit his sphere of influence to Europe in the first place? Apparently, there was more to this part of the world, from the pope's perspective, than just geography.

This assumption can be substantiated by further texts that represent a genuinely religious or theological discourse. In the tenth century, Anskar's *Vita Willehadi* underlined that Charlemagne had been accepted as emperor by the "Catholic church in Europe" (*catholica Europae consistens...ecclesia*) (*BE* 186). Even earlier, in the mid-ninth century, Paschasius Radbertus explained in his *Commentary on the Gospel of St. Matthew*, that the presence of three apostles at the transfiguration of Jesus expressed the fact that redemption through Christ was not limited to Asia but extended to Africa and Europe. This interpretation of a triadic motif as a symbol for the three parts of the *ecumene* was to have a successful career in the following centuries. From the ninth century onwards, numerous triadic motifs that could be found in the biblical texts—Old and New Testament alike—were explained as symbols for the universal calling of the church that existed in all three parts the world.[10]

An early forerunner of this development was the Venerable Bede in the early eighth century, who interpreted the Parable of the Leaven (Matt. 13:33; Luke 13:20–21) as an image for the spread of the Gospel in the entire world that consisted of the three parts Asia, Africa, and Europe. Numerous authors followed this interpretation, including Haymo of Auxerre, Heiricus of Auxerre, and Hincmar of Reims in the ninth century. Later, around 1100, this exegetical approach appears to be well-established: Bruno of Segni (d. 1123) mirrored Bede's interpretation of the Parable of the Leaven, and others, like Anselm of Laon (d. 1117), Hervé de Bourg-Dieu (d. 1150), or Rupert of Deutz (d. 1129) extended this exegetical practice by applying it to several other triadic images. In the early twelfth century, the three magi or Wise Men (based on Matt. 2:1–12) could be interpreted in this sense as well as the three hundred

---

**10** For this and the following paragraph, see Oschema, *Bilder von Europa*, 170–79.

foxes Samson used to burn the corn of the Philistines (Judges 15:4–5) and many others. By means of this genuinely theological discourse, Europe had become part and parcel of religious thinking. At the same time, the exegetical approaches and the motifs they were based on make clear that Europe was not meant to stand alone or even to occupy a special role: its integration into a religiously charged context was fundamentally based on the combination of all three parts of the world. Any meaning Europe might have acquired here relied on its being part of the significant overarching entity.

For a religion that defined its deity as an indivisible trinity, this must have been a very attractive image: such interpretations not only expressed the idea that the Christian religion had spread through the entire world (in the sense of a historical process), they also suggested a world whose tripartite structure reflected the very nature of its own creator. From this perspective, it is understandable that the cartographical traditions in medieval Latin Europe emphasized the tripartite structure of the world in the world-maps, the *mappaemundi*: while some of them took on quite elaborate form, the reductive image of a "T" inscribed in a circle (or an "O") served as an abbreviation for the world from the Central Middle Ages onwards.[11] Like this Western Christian tradition of the "T-O maps," cartographers in the Islamic world also drew on knowledge about the tripartite structure of the world from ancient geographers; however, they rarely relied on this model in their maps.[12]

The period between the ninth and the eleventh centuries is thus characterized by ambivalent findings. While the term Europe was more widely used in texts that concern political discourses in the broadest sense, the word did not take on an explicitly political meaning. In many cases it did not even serve to describe "contemporary" phenomena, but rather to

---

[11] For a useful overview, see David Woodward, "Medieval *Mappaemundi*," in *History of Cartography*, 1:286–370, esp. 296 and 298.

[12] See Mauntel et al., "Mapping Continents," 304–5; cf. also Ducène, *L'Europe et les géographes arabes*.

reflect in a nostalgic mode a former glory that was now lost. From this point of view, the historiographical texts from the tenth and eleventh centuries that had long been treated as the last remnants of a discourse that had seen its heyday in the Carolingian period, appear in a different light. In contrast to their ninth-century forerunners, they seem to express a more positive image that was increasingly focused on the author's present. Apart from this development in historiography, the more strictly ecclesiastical discourse—administrative or genuinely theological—laid the groundwork for later developments that wholeheartedly embraced Europe as a notion that could be meaningfully employed in a religious context.

## Europe, Christianity, and the Church—Possibilities and Cul-de-sacs

The rapprochement between Europe and religion has regrettably been minimized in modern research due to a focus on "political" phenomena. There is no indication that the idea of Europe occupied a meaningful place in the Christian religious discourse from the outset, and thus it is particularly interesting to witness how the notion slowly began to acquire religious overtones. Europe occupied a geographical space that was a priori unfavourable in terms of symbolic interpretation: it had no particular connection with the origins of Christianity, and Christian authors continually stressed the Church's universal vocation. Consequently, the very fact that Christian authors who reflected on their religion and its fundamental texts used the names of the continents at all is highly remarkable and merits a closer look.

Again, one key to understanding this process lies in the inheritance of Greco-Roman Antiquity: early Christian authors were well-versed in this culture (which was basically their own), and it furnished central parameters for the depiction of the world that surrounded them. By the time Christianity became established as a major religion, the model of a tripartite world, the names of the continents, and the mythological traditions that explained them were already entrenched.

Although Christian authors struggled with the parts of this heritage that went against their monotheistic belief, they were forced to use its vocabulary in several contexts, for practical reasons. Still, there remains a profound difference between the use of geographical names for purely administrative purposes (and even here, there is nothing "natural" about the application of existing political or administrative borders for the organization of communities of adherents to a religious group) and the inclusion of these names in religious discourse itself, which invested them with quasi-religious meaning.

Interestingly enough, and in contrast to what one might expect, the explicitly religious dimension soon outpaced the administrative practices: while we have seen a limited number of sources in which the papacy, church administration, and some ecclesiastical practices were associated with Europe, the name of the continent did not acquire a particularly prominent role in these more pragmatic contexts.[13]

In contrast, other practices continued to develop that finally led to a relatively broad and widespread use of the word. A closer look at the tenth- to twelfth-century material reveals that authors of chronicles and annals continued to use the term in a broad variety of contexts. The *Greater Annals of St. Gall*, for example, mentioned an important drought that affected "all the rivers of Europe" in 995 (or 1001); and in the 1070s, Adam of Bremen explained not only that Charlemagne had submitted all the kingdoms of Europe to his rule, thus continuing the Carolingian tradition, he also went on to describe the Slavic city of *Iumne* as the largest city in "Europe."[14] Passages of this kind might appear quite unso-

---

**13** Agostino Paravicini-Bagliani, "La papauté médiévale et le concept de l'Europe," *Académie Royale de Belgique. Bulletin de la Classe des Lettres et des Sciences Morales et Politiques*, ser. 6, 17 (2006): 159–74.

**14** Oschema, *Bilder von Europa*, 166; Volker Scior, *Das Eigene und das Fremde. Identität und Fremdheit in den Chroniken Adams von Bremen, Helmolds von Bosau und Arnolds von Lübeck* (Berlin: Akademie, 2002), 98, 102, and 212–13.

phisticated at first glance, but they are noteworthy in several ways. On the one hand, Adam's text attests to the fact that a Christian author from the northern parts of the empire knew about urban settlements in the regions that were (from his perspective) inhabited by pagans. On the other hand, he explicitly praises a city whose inhabitants, he declared, included several ethnic groups (Slavs, Greek, "Barbarians") who continued to follow pagan traditions despite exposure to Christianity. Adam certainly would have preferred an exclusively Christian community, but he clearly allowed for the existence of non-Christians (as well as orthodox Greek) inside Europe. The implications of this relatively dry localization thus go far beyond the merely "geographical."

In this way, the use of the term often transcended geographical discourse and transported cultural ideas in the broadest sense. This was the case, for example, when Europe became part of migration stories that explained either the origin of populations or the spread of Christianity. The first traces of the story of the migration of the Franks that connect their origins with Troy via the eponymic hero Francio go back to the eighth century.[15] From an early twenty-first century perspective, the fact that a people's own origin story did *not* start with the motif of autochthonic (native-born) development, merits attention. Looking at the early and central medieval *origo gentis* narratives (i.e., stories about the origins of peoples) one detail jumps out: it seems to have been the norm, rather than the exception, for peoples or groups to settle the land they later inhabited after migrating from elsewhere. As modern reconstructions based on archaeological finds and DNA-analysis confirm, the medieval authors of these texts were certainly closer to scientifically verifiable

---

**15** On the *origo gentis*-traditions, see Alheydis Plassmann, *Origo gentis. Identitäts- und Legitimitätsstiftung in früh- und hochmittelalterlichen Herkunftserzählungen* (Berlin: Akademie, 2006), 116–90 (esp. 151). For global comparisons, see *Mythes d'origine dans les civilisations de l'Asie*, ed. Pierre-Sylvain Filliozat and Michel Zink (Leuven: Peeters, 2021).

fact than many of those who circulate right-wing and nationalistic ideas in our own days.[16]

More interesting in the present context, though, is the increasingly "normal" presence of Europe in several migration stories, which were continuously elaborated upon in the Central Middle Ages. While the earliest texts about the Goths and the Huns already mentioned their coming "into Europe" from beyond, Troy played an increasingly important role as the "cradle of the peoples" in the minds of medieval authors, leading to a myriad of such narratives. The *Miracula s. Genulfi*, for example, probably written in the eleventh century, explained that the Sicambrians were the descendants not of those Trojans who followed Aeneas to Italy, but rather of the descendants of Antenor who crossed the Don, thereby entering Europe, and allegedly arrived in Pannonia (*BE* 216). The anonymous author repeats motifs long present in the equally anonymous *Liber historiae Francorum* in the mid-eighth history. But while the *Liber historiae Francorum* explicitly situated Troy in Asia and mentioned the Sicambrians' movements towards the West, it did not explicitly mention Europe.

Nor did the authors who invented traditions for their city, their region, or their people always limit themselves to a Trojan connection. At Trier, for example, the anonymous authors of the first version of the *Gesta Treverorum*, went even further when they explained that their city had been founded by Trebeta, a son of King Ninus who fled the advances of his stepmother Semiramis by crossing the Mediterranean—and so had migrated from Asia to Europe. At that time, the author explains, this part of the world was still unpeopled and Trebeta established Treves (Trier) as the first city and the "head of Europe" (*capud Europae*) (*BE* 167). With this creative invention, the *Gesta Treverorum* not only directly connected their

---

**16** For popular presentations on how the diversity of genetic material reflects the mixing of populations, see Johannes Krause and Thomas Trappe, *Die Reise unserer Gene. Eine Geschichte über uns und unsere Vorfahren* (Berlin: Propyläen, 2019), and Alistair Moffat and Jim Wilson, *The Scots: A Genetic Journey* (Edinburgh: Birlinn, 2011).

city's origin back to the bible, it also furnished material for claiming that their city was older than Rome! In addition, the *capud Europae* formula seems to imply that Europe meant more than just a geographical notion to the *Gesta*'s author(s).

Origin stories of this kind mostly concerned phenomena that can by and large be described as "secular," but they also demonstrate the continuing use of the notion of Europe, one that had become part of (mostly clerical) authors' active vocabulary. Whereas earlier historiographers, such as Frechulf of Lisieux in the ninth century, had mainly relied on older material when they used the name of the continent, authors from the tenth century onwards started doing so independently of sources from Late Antiquity. This observation is important since it demonstrates that theologians who introduced the continent's name into their texts were not entirely cut off from other developments, but rather represent a different facet of a shared culture.

Theologians did, in fact, increasingly use the notion of Europe. If Bede was innovative when he interpreted the three magi in the early eighth century as the three parts of the world that had come together in the Christian faith, by the Central Middle Ages the idea he coined (which relied on older traditions) had become quite common. We find it in the works of Bruno of Segni, Rupert of Deutz, and many others, for instance. But theologians not only seized the opportunity of triadic motifs found in the biblical texts (as we explained above), they also described the historical process of the dissemination of the Christian faith by referring to the continents. This slowly but progressively contributed to establishing a concept charged with religious connotations.

We have seen the first steps towards this development in Sulpicius Severus's and Venantius Fortunatus's description of St. Martin's overwhelming holiness, echoed by Alcuin in his *Carmen 194* around 800. From the eighth century onwards, the regions where the apostles were active were increasingly identified in detailed geographical terms. While Bede merely commented on the addressees of St. Peter's first epistle, underlining that they were all Greek and in Asia (though there was another Bithynia in Europe), in the late ninth century the Irish recluse Dungal explained that St. Andrew was sent to the Parthians and St. John the Younger to the Ephesians so that they might evangelize Europe and Asia (this logic does not accord with reality, since Ephesus lies on the Western shore of Asia Minor). From the early ninth century onwards, some texts explicitly highlighted the activities of Sts. Peter and Paul "in Europe," which they "illuminated with their preaching." According to Walahfrid Strabo, for example, Paul's journey from Ephesus to Macedonia not only brought the apostle from Asia to Europe: the author also underlined that crossing the continental border had actually been Paul's intention (*BE* 183).

In this development, the history of the Christian religion and its dissemination converged with its geographical framework, investing the latter with religious meaning. The formula *capud Europae* that Atto of Vercelli used to describe Illyria is ambivalent: it might simply mean that this region was the first that one enters after crossing the border between the continents. However, the context also implies a symbolic dimension, since this was the region that was first touched by St. Paul's activities in this part of the world. Later, the *caput Europae*-formula was increasingly used in connection with Rome, whose excellence resulted from the fact that it was home to two apostles' graves (*BE* 184). In addition, Notker the Stammerer explained that the church of San Pietro in Vinculo had been the first church that St. Peter built in this part of the world.

These motifs were seized upon by the popes in the Central Middle Ages. In a letter to patriarch Michael of Constantinople, Pope Leo IX explicitly underlined the role of St. Peter as well as the activities of Sts. Paul and Barnabas in the evangelization of Europe and Africa in order to justify the universal position of Rome, which he called the "head of the world and the ruler over the peoples" (*BE* 185). Slowly but surely the continent had become a new home for the Christian religion: Christianity's origins might well have resided in Asia—and this idea remained present throughout the Middle Ages—but the heads of the Catholic church and numerous Latin authors justified a particularly important position for the church in Europe through biblical exegesis. The vocation of the church remained universal, but the seat of the supreme authority had been transferred to Europe, more precisely to Rome (at least this was the point of view held by the Roman popes and many Latin Christian authors).

According to Peter the Venerable, the Latin church had received the Gospel from St. Peter, and the Greek church from St. Paul—and Europe inherited both apostles' tradition. While this image stressed the union of Latin and Greek Christianity, the authority of St. Peter frequently took the prize. In the thirteenth century, Jacques de Voragine used the name Europe only once in his widely read *Legenda aurea*, namely to explain why St. Peter had three feast-days in the ecclesiastical year: he played a universal role because he had been active as a prelate in Asia, Europe, and Africa.

Seen against this backdrop, it would be a mistake to conclude that Europe did not play any role at all in the eyes of the Church. While the cited texts did not dominate the day-to-day dealings of the Church and its members, they do reflect widespread ideas and assumptions. The potential that arose from these more general ideas about Europe and its role in the Latin Christian worldview can be witnessed in the tormented period around 1100. Following the call to help their Christian brothers in the East (made by Pope Urban II at Clermont in 1095) several armies took up the cross and set off for the Holy Land, effectively succeeding in conquering Jerusalem in July 1099. In the course (and the wake) of this development, a number of principalities in the Levant found themselves in the hands of Latin Christian rulers. Even more importantly, several institutions, like the recently founded Order of the Knights Hospitaller, held possessions on the European and the Asian side of the Mediterranean. In this situation, the question of an appropriate and useful terminology arose.[17]

---

**17** For a general overview, see for instance, Christopher Tyerman, *God's War. A New History of the Crusades* (Cambridge, MA: Belknap, 2006).

In the long run, most authors began to speak of territories or possessions on "this side of the sea" (*cismarinus*) and on "the other side" (*ultramarinus*), thus making the Mediterranean the central criterion. However, this terminology was not without alternatives: indeed, several papal documents used the names of the parts of the world to describe the new reality. An early privilege that did so was issued by Pope Paschalis II (1099–1118) on February 15, 1113. Answering the request of Gerard, the founder of the Knights Hospitaller, Paschalis took the hospital in Jerusalem under the protection of the apostolic see and confirmed the order's possessions "on the other side and on this side of the sea, that is in Asia and in Europe."[18]

Earlier confirmations of the order's possessions issued by the kings of Jerusalem did not contain such references to the continents—so the specification seems to have been introduced by the papal chancery. In fact, the charter for the Knights Hospitaller was not the first papal diploma that did so. In 1099 or 1100, Paschalis confirmed a privilege that his predecessor Urban II had issued for Bishop Stephen of Huesca in 1098. In it, Urban referred to the Christians' fight against the Turks in Asia and against the "Moors" in Europe. It thus seems that the events around 1100 led the popes—or at least their chancery personnel—to experiment with different concepts.

Further documents issued by Paschalis II point in the same direction. A charter to an unnamed addressee (possibly the archbishop of Split), underlined that it was against the "custom of the apostolic see and of all of Europe" that an archbishop consecrated bishops or celebrated synods before he had received the pallium. In a letter to King Henry I of England, Paschalis explained in 1105 that the successors of Peter and Paul had evangelized the entire "community of Europe" (*Europae universitas*). In 1113, the *inscriptio* of a letter of recommendation for the papal legate Arcelin addressed the "bishops, abbots, princes (*proceres*), and all the other faithful in Europe." An analogous formula also appears in a letter by Calixtus II

---

**18** For the material in this and the following paragraphs, see Oschema, *Bilder von Europa*, 195–200.

(1119–1124), but this document might be a forgery. Shortly after the conclusion of the concordat of Worms in 1122, however, Calixtus, did write to Emperor Henry V (1105/6–1125) that the rivalries between pope and emperor had brought discord and detriment to the "faithful of Europe" (*Europe fidelibus*).

Paschalis visibly experimented with formulas that were quite extraordinary. His reasons for doing so are difficult to reconstruct: the new perspectives opened by the First Crusade and the conquest of Jerusalem certainly played a role, as did the intensified and confrontational contacts with Byzantium and Orthodox Christianity, and the fact that Paschalis was confronted with a number of rivals in his claim for the apostolic see. Taken together, these factors likely created a situation in which the popes had an interest in underlining their authority over the church in Europe (and possibly beyond, as is attested through the charter for the Knights Hospitaller).

In the long run, these moments of creative experimentation enjoyed only limited success. Although the privilege for the Knights Hospitaller continued to be confirmed by succeeding popes and the distinction between Asia and Europe was duly copied for several decades, in most other documents this distinction was soon replaced by the alternative *cismarinus* versus *transmarinus*. As to the "church in Europe," the popes that followed Paschalis II and Calixtus II did not pick up the concept with any urgency. Several sources do describe synods as gatherings of the clergy in Europe, but these are mostly historiographic texts. Nevertheless we can see that the papacy, in the decades around 1100, did experiment with the notion of Europe, and the circumstances of this period might thus have combined to provide a "window of opportunity" for the potential of the notion.

## The Stability of Knowledge: Europe and the Description of the World

As we have seen, the use of the notion of Europe continued to develop during the Central Middle Ages. While the application in historiographic and panegyric contexts might express a certain political charge, the appearance of the term in a (relatively small) number of papal documents in the period around 1100 attests to its potential in a situation of "geopolitical" change. Though the specific context rapidly ebbed away, its transient appearance is a testament to the notion's potential in the eyes of contemporaries.

Beyond developments that express the malleability of the use of the term, numerous other texts demonstrate to which degree Europe had become the focal point of canonical knowledge. Towards the twelfth century, the erudite of Latin Europe were well acquainted with the myth of Europa and it is safe to assume that most clerical authors knew the basic outlines of the story—especially since this period witnessed a growing interest in Ovid, whose works had become part of the standard curriculum. Indeed, the anonymous author of the *Eupolemius*, an epic poem on biblical stories that dates to the eleventh or early twelfth century, does not mention the princess Europa explicitly, but speaks instead of the "daughter of Agenor" (*Agenore nata*), indicating that he expected his readers to understand this allusion (*BE* 201).

In the twelfth and thirteenth centuries, Europa's story can be found in numerous variations in historiographical texts, encyclopaedic works, and other sources. Bartholomaeus Anglicus mentions her in his *De proprietatibus rerum*, where he presents Agenor as the king of "Africa" (*rex Libyæ*), narrates the abduction of Europa by Jupiter, and identifies the princess as the person who gave her name to this part of the world. A few years later, Vincent of Beauvais included a similar choice of information in his *Speculum naturale* and his *Speculum historiale*. While some details of the presentation could occasionally vary—several authors, among them Petrus Comestor, identified Europa as the daughter of Phoenix instead of Agenor—the central elements had become quite stable. That some of the remaining uncertainties lingered on for some time can be seen in Giovanni Boccaccio's *De mulieribus claris* (ca. 1361/62), where both affiliations are mentioned. At the same time, the author clearly expressed his preference for the Agenor-variant; the mainstream view. As he put it: *verum longe plures eam Ageno-*

*ris, Phenicum regis, genitam dicunt* (in truth, many more say that
she was born of Agenor, the king of the Phoenicians, *BE* 203).

Depending on the nature and focus of the work in question, individual authors presented a differing degree of detail.
The bishop of Tyre, William of Tyre, who wrote his *Cronica*
in the late twelfth century, included an elaborate version of
Europa's story, in which he identified Agenor as the king of
Tyre and tied Europa's fate to the history of "his" city. Tyre's
geographical location and William's trajectory between Latin
Western Europe and the Levant might also explain why he
repeatedly insisted on the Hellespont as the border between
Asia and Europe.

Interestingly, Latin authors of this period were not yet
keen to develop a genuinely Christian interpretation of the
myth of Europa, and it was only by the early fourteenth century that allegorical texts tried to develop "moralizing" Christianized interpretations of the mythological motifs found in
Ovid's works. In the anonymous *Ovide moralisé* as well as in
Petrus Berchorius's *Reductorium morale*, Europa becomes an
allegory for the human soul that is safely transported over
the rough sea of worldly existence by its saviour Jesus Christ
(in the form of the bull) (*BE* 483–84). From this moment on,
Europa also appeared more often in images, for instance in
book illuminations. However, these allegorical interpretations
focused exclusively on the Christian reading of the myth itself
and made no attempt to draw any conclusions whatsoever
that might have situated it in a broader context. In this sense,
the moralizing interpretations did not contribute decisively to
the ideas that became connected with Europe.

Based on earlier texts, works from the Central Middle
Ages also continued to mention King Europs:[19] he appears in
Otto of Freising's chronicle as well as in Irish texts of the *Sex
aetates sunt mundi*-tradition. The authors were often content
to merely mention this figure, whom they identified as the
king of the Sycionians (or sometimes the Scythians, as in the
Irish *Book of Leccan*). In most cases, Europs appears along-

---

**19** See above, chap. 2, n. 6.

side Europa when it comes to explaining the origin of the continent's name—only rarely did an author exclusively mention Europs: Albert of Stade (d. 1264), for example, who identified him as the name-giver, is part of this minority tradition, to which only a few, albeit sometimes famous, authors belong, including Gossouin de Metz and his *Image du Monde*. Towards the end of the Middle Ages, authors of scientific works seem to have cultivated a predilection for Europs, as is witnessed by the astrologer Louis de Langle (d. 1463/1464) in his *De figura seu imagine mundi*.

The most important context in which knowledge about Europe had become canonical was certainly geographical. Based on an uninterrupted tradition since Late Antiquity, countless authors repeated what could already be read in Isidore of Seville's *Etymologies*: the entire known *ecumene* was divided into three parts called Asia, Europe, and Africa. When Honorius Augustodunensis wrote his *Imago mundi* in the early twelfth century, he echoed exactly this image—explaining that "the habitable zone that we inhabit" (*que a nobis incolitur*) was thus tripartite, with Asia occupying the part from the north via the east to the south, while Europe extended from the west to the north and Africa from the south to the west.

This rudimentary, but fundamental information was often followed by a detailed outline of the different regions, including the individual parts of the world. The organization of the resulting presentations could vary, and they provided different categories of information. One of the most elaborate examples that exerted enormous influence on medieval authors was the first book of Orosius's *History Against the Pagans*, written in the early fifth century. In this first part of his work, the author set the scene by providing a more or less complete geographical outline of the entire *ecumene* as known in the Roman Empire around 400 CE—including *Taprobane* (Sri Lanka) and the "Chinese ocean" (*oceanus Sericus*) (bk. 1, chap. 2, §§13, 47). Honorius Augustodunensis's overview was much shorter, but it followed a similar logic: having listed the main regions of Asia, starting with the earthly paradise in the utmost east and the four rivers that flow from it, via India, Mesopotamia, Syria, etc., Honorius begins his description of Europe with Scythia and what he calls *Germania superior*. After this and the neighbouring *Germania inferior*, he describes Greece, Italy, France (*Gallia*), Spain, and Britain, before finally turning to Africa.

By the early twelfth century, Europe had become the "third part of the world" for most authors, though the structure of the *orbis* could sometimes be described according to different models. In the middle of the thirteenth century, for example, Albertus Magnus distinguished the four cardinal directions—and had quite a difficult time bringing this mathematical approach into unison with the more geographical tripartite structure. Yet another model put the accent on climes—distinguishing separate parallel climate zones (most often five of seven) between the equator and the poles.

The different models can also be illustrated with the world-maps that have been preserved in steadily growing numbers from the twelfth century onwards.[20] While many follow only one model, numerous examples express their makers' desire to combine the different models in one single picture. One of the earliest examples has survived in an eleventh-century copy of Macrobius's *Commentary on the Somnium Scipionis*.

The circular picture (Fig. 2) shows the known *ecumene* in a semicircle that occupies the upper half of the *orbis*, while the "antecumene" can be seen in the lower half. Both parts are subdivided into climatical zones that mirror each other. They share the torrid zone around the equator, which is followed by a temperate (and thus habitable) zone and then a cold one around the poles. More detailed representations from later centuries, like Louis de Langle's map (Fig. 3), show that each of the hemispheres could be further subdivided into as much as seven different zones.

---

**20** While earlier maps are known, they tend to be less elaborate; in addition, the quantity of known maps increases dramatically from the twelfth century onwards. For indicative numbers, see Woodward, "Medieval Mappaemundi," 1:298.

Fig. 2: World-map from Macrobius, *Commentary on the Somnium Scipionis*, eleventh century. Oxford, Bodleian Library, MS D'Orville 77, fol. 100r. Digital Bodleian, photo: © Bodleian Libraries, University of Oxford; licence CC-BY-NC 4.0.

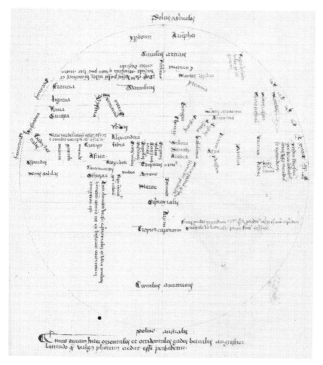

Fig. 3: World-map from Louis de Langle,
*De figura seu imagine mundi*, mid-fifteenth century.
St. Gallen, Kantonsbibliothek Vadiana,
VadSlg MS 427, fol. 125r.

What is particularly noteworthy in the present context,
however, is that the maker of the Macrobian map in Oxford
already tried to project the tripartite structure of the *ecumene*
onto the more abstract climate model. Consequently, the
northern half of the map appears more structured, while the
southern half contains an undifferentiated landmass. There
were many debates about the nature of this part of the *orbis*:
while some thought that it might only be occupied water,

others argued for land.[21] In the end, nothing could really be known for certain, since the hot zone around the equator was imagined to be insurmountable. Lambert of St. Omer made this point quite explicit in the world map he included in his *Liber Floridus* (ca. 1120) (Fig. 4): "the temperate part of the southern half is unknown to the sons of Adam."

By Lambert's time, Europe had become the third part of the world and the texts that continued to mention the existence of a "small Europe" (i.e., the Thracian province of Late Antiquity) became increasingly rare. Examples which mention this *minor Europa*, however, include famous works like Gervase of Tilbury's *Otia imperialia* and Ralph of Diceto's *Abbreviationes Chronicorum*. More important than this distinction seems to have been the consensus on the continent's borders. On this subject there was hardly any debate, but nearly every text that described Europe or the *ecumene* explicitly mentioned the borders and their place. In contrast to the situation in Greek and Roman Antiquity, Latin authors from the Central Middle Ages onwards were almost unanimous. A brief but representative formula can be found in the *Dragmaticon Philosophiae* by William of Conches (d. after 1145): "Europe ends towards the East at the Don, towards the South at the Mediterranean, towards the West at the Atlantic Sea, towards the North at the frigid zone" (*BE* 210–11). Honorius Augustodunensis went into more detail when he identified the start of the northern border at the *Rifei montes* (notoriously hard to identify) and then followed the Don until the *Palus Maeotis* (i.e., the Black Sea). This picture is confirmed in numerous texts and maps from the Central Middle Ages onwards.

Only in very exceptional cases did individual authors propose alternative views, and these are often hard to explain:

---

**21** See Anna-Dorothee von den Brincken, *Fines Terrae. Die Enden der Erde und der vierte Kontinent auf mittelalterlichen Weltkarten* (Hanover: Hahn, 1992); Alfred Hiatt, *Terra Incognita. Mapping the Antipodes before 1600* (London: British Library, 2008); see also the short presentation in Seb Falk, *The Light Ages. A Medieval Journey of Discovery* (London: Allen Lane, 2020), 90–96.

according to Gossouin of Metz, for example, the Alps separated Europe from Africa. This unique concept might have resulted from his desire to present a historically oriented image of geography, in which the arena of contemporary politics had shifted to the regions north of the Alps.[22] Writing in the early fifteenth century, the chronicler Ulrich Richental presented an equally singular, but more understandable model: in his *Chronicle of the Council of Constance*, he located Constantinople and Athens in Africa, which allowed him to implicitly depict Europe as the realm of Latin Christianity (*BE* 212).

However, Gossouin and Ulrich were exceptional and did not rely on detailed discussions about the physical nature of the borders. Even when individual authors had a better first-hand knowledge of the regions where the borders were traditionally held to be, the effects of this empirical information remained limited for a long time. The Franciscan William of Rubruck, for example, one of the first mendicant friars who travelled to the Mongols in the mid-thirteenth century, explicitly rectified what had long been taught about the Caspian Sea: while Isidore of Seville described it as being open towards the Northern Ocean, William clearly stated this was not the case. When he reached the Don, however, he merely commented that this river separated Europe from Asia—though he noted only a bit further along in his text that the Volga was the largest river he had ever seen (*BE* 216). Yet he did not extrapolate from this to call into question what he had learnt beforehand. It was not before the fifteenth century and the work of Fra Mauro that more explicit doubts were formulated. The famous mapmaker-monk from Venice mentioned the differences between the "ancient" authors, such as Pomponius Mela or Ptolemy, and the "modern" ones, whom he did not identify. Concerning the Eastern border of Europe, Fra

---

**22** Georg Jostkleigrewe, "L'espace entre tradition et innovation. La géographie symbolique du monde et son adaptation par Gossouin de Metz," in *Construction de l'espace au Moyen Âge: pratiques et représentations. XXXVIIe Congrès de la SHMES* (Paris: Publications de la Sorbonne, 2007), 369–78 at 375–77.

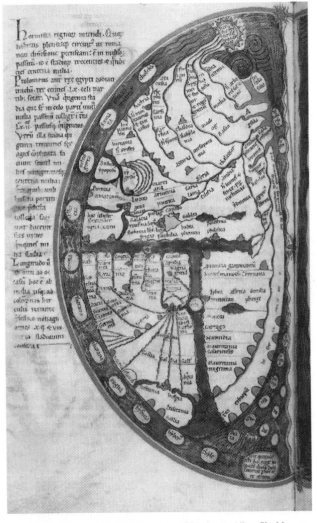

Fig. 4: World-map from Lambert of St. Omer, *Liber Floridus*, ca. 1120. Herzog August Bibliothek Wolfenbüttel, Guelf. 1 Gud. lat., fols. 69v–70r; licence CC BY-SA 3.0 DE.

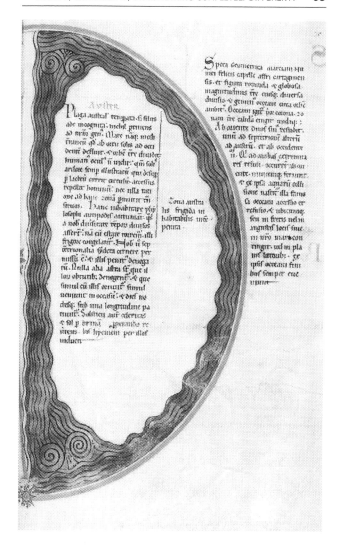

Mauro explained that the Volga offered a much more suitable geographical boundary than the Don, but he gave no clear stance. Instead, he declared the entire problem to be of only secondary importance and referred his readers quite vaguely to the "authority of the more authentic [authors]...."[23]

All in all, the borders of the continent were well known in theory, though our authors mostly remained unfamiliar with the actual lands in the East until at least the thirteenth century. This absence of detailed discussions (or explanations) did not mean that the entire question was meaningless. Quite the contrary, since central and late medieval authors who wrote about the Don, the Hellespont, or the Bosporus would mention that these places marked the border between Europe and Asia. William of Tyre did so repeatedly in his "Chronicle," as did numerous other texts that described travels from Europe to Asia: the *Chronicle* of Helinand of Froidmont (d. ca. 1230), for example, relates that Archbishop Maurilius of Rouen had been transported in a vision to Jerusalem—and even describes this imaginary travel as a journey from Europe to Asia (*BE* 215).

The border regions were not only frequently mentioned and clearly identified; they also acquired a specific set of connotations (see further in chap. 5 below). Based on the idea that Europe had somehow become a sort of refuge or homeland to Latin Christianity—that is, the "real" Christian Church in the eyes of these authors—the crossing of the borders by peoples who were perceived to be "enemies of the faith" became synonymous with dangerous threats. Moreover, the eastern, and especially the northeastern, borders were frequently perceived as particularly fearful regions where dangerous peoples or even monsters could be found. According to Godfrey of Viterbo (d. ca. 1191/1192), the Huns had originally come from the regions neighbouring the *Maeotides Paludes*—that is, on the border between Asia and Europe—where they had been supposedly born from the union of incubi and prostitutes (*BE* 127). According to other texts and

---

**23** See Christoph Mauntel, "Fra Mauro's View on the Boring Question of Continents," *Peregrinations* 6, no. 3 (2018): 54–77.

maps alike, these regions were the lands where Alexander the Great had enclosed the monstrous peoples of Gog and Magog, who would break loose during the end-times. Regions that were geographically on the margins—always from the perspective of the authors—were imagined as fertile homes of monstrous beings and threats (see chap. 5, n. 33 below).

It should now be clear that by the twelfth century Europe and its borders had taken on implications and connotations that went far beyond the "merely geographic." Although most of the passages where the continent was mentioned remain quite brief and "dry" at first sight, their sheer number and the multitude of contexts in which they appeared are testimony to these changing cultural meanings. The question remains: do these developments also imply more concrete ideas concerning a "European character" (as seen from the inside)? In this respect, the image provided by our sources is somewhat difficult to gauge, as the overwhelming majority of texts tends to reflect the consolidated knowledge that the medieval world had inherited from Antiquity. Nevertheless, new uses developed in some cases.

Possibly building on the identification of Europe as a meaningful "space of resonance" for the reputation of saints, a notion that developed from the seventh century onwards, some texts from the eleventh and twelfth centuries started to invest a small set of rulers with "European honours." While the tradition surrounding Charlemagne slowly gave way to more universal epithets, Alexander the Great began to make his appearance as a universal ruler on the basis that he had acquired dominion over all three continents: Honorius Augustodunensis's *Elucidarium*, for example, spoke of "the great Alexander, who subjugated Asia, Africa, and Europe" (*BE* 221). The same idea surfaces in numerous other texts, including Thomas of Kent's version of the Alexander-romance and the German version of the *Elucidarius*, among others. John of Salisbury (d. 1180), for example, described an omen on the day of Alexander's birth in his *Policraticus*: two eagles sat down on his father's palace, indicating that the new-born was destined to rule over Europe and Asia (*BE* 221).

Another ruler who acquired a European dimension from the twelfth century onwards, albeit in mostly negative terms, was the legendary King Arthur. According to Geoffrey of Monmouth (d. ca. 1155), the successful ruler and his expansive career soon started to inspire fear amongst neighbouring rulers, and he aspired to subjugate all of Europe—a motif that had some success in later centuries, since Matthew Paris, Robert of Gloucester, Jean de Wavrin, and others repeated it. It seems that this idea of "rule over all of Europe" was mainly cultivated by English authors, who might simply have understood it as any expansion of authority on the continent. In addition, the motif mostly appeared in relation to rulers from a distant and legendary past. Another tradition also began in the twelfth century that used the motif as a negative projection: the aspiration to European rulership was frequently ascribed to non-Christian rulers who allegedly tried to conquer and subjugate the continent.[24]

Positive ideas could be connected with Europe too. In this sense, Gerald of Wales (d. ca. 1223) emphasized that King Henry II of England (1154–1189) "illuminated" three parts of Europe by marrying off his three daughters. In addition, Gerald explained, all the princes of the world, "Christians and Heathen alike, from Asia and from Europe" allegedly sent envoys to Henry (*BE* 225). Such informal influence extended across the continent could be used to praise a ruler's position. Finally, Europe generally became established as a frame of reference to permit someone to be praised as the biggest, most admired, or the best "in Europe": for instance, an anonymous chronicle from twelfth-century York explained that Bede's writings were "admired by all of Europe"; the castle of Devizes is repeatedly described as the "most magnificent in Europe"; William of Newburgh called Rouen "one of the most famous cities in Europe" (*BE* 229). So, by the twelfth century, Europe had become a sort of "household expression" that could be meaningfully

---

**24** See Oschema, "No 'Emperor of Europe'."

employed in a number of different contexts, at least as a frame of reference. These texts demonstrate, however, that most authors did not yet connect more tangible, concrete, or far-reaching ideas with the continent—but this was soon to change.

Chapter 5

# Our Last Hope? Entangling Europe and Christianity in the Late Middle Ages

The preceding overview on the situation by the twelfth century focused on the development of older traditions, but afterwards authors in the later Middle Ages did more than just transmit and elaborate on inherited knowledge: they also learned to integrate the continent into contexts and discourses where its use was far from obvious (especially concerning religious questions). In addition, the sheer number of texts that referred to Europe, even when they did so only briefly, demonstrates that Europe had become a relatively prominent element in the authors' worldview. While some ancient debates had been laid to rest (e.g., on the number of the continents or on the borders that separated them), new practices developed. The papacy (or its chancery) experimented with the notion in the years around 1100, and Europe appeared in numerous texts as a "space of resonance" or comparison for diverse phenomena. Most importantly, many authors explicitly identified the borders and the surrounding regions, especially between Europe and Asia, as a relevant and significant entity, and crossing those borders became a noteworthy act that was repeatedly mentioned in our sources. This chapter builds on these observations and inverts the perspective. Taking the eleventh and twelfth centuries as its starting point, it identifies central developments that characterized the uses of the notion of Europe towards the later Middle Ages.

## Under Threat: Discovering Europe in Struggles against Saracens, Mongols, and Turks

Medievalists have often observed that, even in the absence of a concrete idea of Europe, specific contexts nevertheless triggered use of the notion. Indeed, having the word to hand, central and late medieval authors were quite capable and willing to employ it whenever it strengthened their argument. Accordingly, Bernd Schneidmüller has dubbed the notion of Europe as an "on-call term" (*Abrufbegriff*) that could be used at will, even though it played no essential role in the everyday workings of society and politics.[1] Examples of this phenomenon can be found in contexts where authors described or commented upon a—perceived or real—menace from "outside."

Constellations of this kind might appear to be relatively improbable at first glance: as we have seen, the Christianization of the European peoples, who thus accepted a religion of Asian origin, was largely accomplished (at least superficially) by the end of the first millennium—and a considerable number of texts emphasized this very fact when they described the works of the apostles. In addition, the origin stories of many peoples also relied on the motif of migration: in their own eyes and their own histories, most people lived where they were because they had come from someplace else and had either cultivated or conquered another land. Migration and movement were therefore an integral part of their imaginary—why then, should crossing a continental border be particularly noteworthy?

As the following examples reveal, any interpretation of this phenomenon must reckon with an increasing proximity between Europe and the Church (or Catholic Christianity) from the eleventh century onwards. Already in the early medieval period, individual texts could refer to the "church in Europe," but now this motif became widespread and charged with a specific sense in the context and aftermath of Pope Urban II's crusading call.

---

[1] Schneidmüller, "Die mittelalterlichen Konstruktionen," 6–16.

Unfortunately, the original text of the sermon that Urban delivered at Clermont in November 1095 has not come down to us, and the acts of the synod that preceded it do not mention the speech. Several chroniclers, however, provide us with different versions of the event. We will never be able to reconstruct the original wording with absolute certainty, but we do know that the speech and its delivery had a huge effect:[2] over the course of the following year, several "waves" of people that we now conveniently label "crusaders" (although the word did not then exist), left their homes in the western parts of Europe. Some successfully conquered and occupied new territories in the Levant, including Jerusalem, and since the territories in question had once been under Christian rule, they claimed that their actions amounted to a reconquest.

What is noteworthy for us is that Europe probably did not play any particular role in Urban's speech, which was, according to the sources, dominated by religious categories: the version given by Fulcher of Chartres, for example, underlines the need to fight the "infidel" in order to help the "Christians" in the East (it does not even mention Jerusalem). Only a few decades later, the English monk and chronicler William of Malmesbury (d. ca. 1143) gave a more embellished and detailed version of Urban's speech. In it, the pope explicitly drew a picture of a tripartite earth that had once been entirely Christian though the regions of Asia and Africa had fallen into the hands of the "enemies of God" (*inimicos Dei*), leaving Christians to merely rule over Europe, which was also home to "barbarian" peoples. Urban supposedly also declared that in "our small part of the world" (*nostri mundi portiunculam*), Christians were now threatened with war by "Turks" and "Saracens" (*BE* 267–69).

---

**2** Christof T. Maier, "Konflikt und Kommunikation. Neues zum Kreuzzugsaufruf Urbans II.," in *Jerusalem im Hoch- und Spätmittelalter. Konflikte und Konfliktbewältigung—Vorstellung und Vergegenwärtigungen*, ed. Dieter Bauer, Klaus Herbers, and Nikolas Jaspert (Frankfurt/M.: Campus, 2001), 12–30.

Although William of Malmesbury's version of Urban's speech is certainly not close to the real wording, it nevertheless provides important evidence as one of the earliest witnesses of a motif that Johannes Helmrath has dubbed "*angulus*-syndrome" in his work on the perception of the Ottoman expansion in the late Middle Ages.[3] At the heart of this motif is the idea that Christianity was menaced by external adversaries while its own space had been reduced to a small part of the world. This motif proved effective as motivation, and it was to have a long afterlife. At the same time, it is noticeable that the notion invited authors to present situations that they deemed critical and dangerous in terms of geographic units and borders. After all, Urban's speech was a "crusade sermon" that sought to persuade people to give up their daily life, go on a dangerous journey from which many would not return, and fight against religious adversaries. Urban's attempt to motivate a crowd of listeners through the enumeration of Syria, Armenia, Asia Minor with its provinces Bithynia, Phrygia, Galatia, and so forth, as the "enemies of God"—according to William of Malmesbury—is far from obvious as a technique. Further, in William's presentation of the speech, Europe became all that remained of the once entirely "Christian" world—and the part that "we Christians" inhabited was deemed all too small: *Tertium mundi clima restat Europa, cuius quantulam partem inhabitamus Christiani!*

On this basis, William introduced yet another motif.[4] One tenet of late twentieth-century medievalists was that the crusades, which some considered to represent a "European movement" *par excellence*, was not framed in European terms

---

**3** Helmrath, "Pius II. und die Türken," 97, adopting the expression from Mertens, "Europäischer Friede," 52–53.

**4** For this paragraph see Oschema, *Bilder von Europa*, 270–74; Klaus Oschema, "L'idée d'Europe et les croisades (XIe–XVe siècles)," in *Relations, échanges et transferts en Occident au cours des derniers siècles du Moyen Âge. Hommage à Werner Paravicini*, ed. Bernard Guenée and Jean-Marie Moeglin (Paris: Académie des Inscriptions et Belles-Lettres, 2010), 51–86.

by medieval authors; but this is not entirely true. According to William, "nearly all of Europe" went on an expedition to Asia, and he explicitly characterized what we now call the First Crusade as the "expedition to Asia that, in our days, Europe moved against the Turks." It must be said, though, that William appears to have cultivated an unusual predilection for the notion of "Europe": the term appears no less than thirteen times in his *Gesta regum Anglorum*. His formulation concerning the crusades found imitators: Guy de Bazoches (d. after 1203) repeated it and through his work it made its way into the *Chronicle* of Alberic of Troisfontaines (d. after 1252). In Italy, Romuald of Salerno (d. 1181) also saw Christians "from all of Europe" (*ex omni Europa*) go to Jerusalem after Urban's speech, and Henry of Huntingdon (d. ca. 1157) described the crusade as a movement of "many dukes [or military leaders] of Europe" (*multis ducibus Europe*). Taken together, these texts do not necessarily mean that the crusades were mainly perceived as a conflict between Europe and Asia, but they do demonstrate that it could be framed as such.

To understand the logic behind the expressions, we should acknowledge the pervasiveness of the "*angulus*-motif" in William of Malmesbury. From the early twelfth century, some authors started to perceive—and to describe—Europe as the region that had become the homeland of Christians. This does not mean, that Europe and Christianity had become synonymous—quite the contrary: the prevalence of references to Christians and Christianity clearly expresses the emphasis that was put on genuinely religious categories. While Europe had acquired religious connotations, Christianity always kept its universal outlook. Yet another English chronicler, this time from the late twelfth century, makes this explicit: for William of Newburgh (d. 1198), Jerusalem had been conquered by Christian troops that "had come from Europe." And in doing so, these Christians—the "peoples of Europe" and so descendants of Japheth—fulfilled the prophecy of Genesis 9:27: "Japheth shall dwell in the tents of Shem." Only a few decades after the conquest, Christians in the kingdom of Jerusalem were threatened by Saladin and sought help amongst the "princes in Europe"; still, they were expelled from Jerusalem after just eighty-seven years (*BE* 272).

These examples demonstrate the religious and political connotations of Europe in the context of the crusades, which went far beyond a neutral or objective description of the events. This effect was not limited to the crusades, which relied upon an imaginary threat to Europe that led to aggressive military actions and to real expansion beyond the continent's borders.

The quoted passages have focused on the crusades to the Levant; however, there was another arena that saw more successful Christian military actions. In the context of the so-called Spanish "Reconquista" (a highly problematic and ideologically charged term),[5] the notion of Europe also played a role, but only from a relatively late moment onwards. The earliest historiographic evidence from the kingdom of Asturia (in the northeast of the Iberian peninsula) stressed the difference between Christians and non-Christians or simply presented the events using the terminology of military conflicts. This changed perceptibly in the thirteenth century: Rodrigo Jiménez de Rada (d. 1247), archbishop of Toledo from 1209, in his *Historia de Rebus Hispaniae,* explicitly focused on some of the "inhabitants of Europe" (*incolis Europe*) (bk. 1, chap. 2), more precisely the Goths who migrated in devastating excursions through Asia and Europe before settling down in Spain. The key framework for his history was the geographical unit of Spain, a region that was inhabited by a series of different peoples attracted by its wealth.

Particularly remarkable in this text is the description of the battle of Las Navas de Tolosa (1212), one of the decisive moments in the expansive military campaigns of the Castilian kings. On this occasion, King Alfonso VIII had assembled

---

**5** See Nikolas Jaspert, "'Reconquista.' Interdependenzen und Tragfähigkeit eines wertekategorialen Deutungsmusters," in *Christlicher Norden—Muslimischer Süden: Ansprüche und Wirklichkeiten von Christen, Juden und Muslimen auf der Iberischen Halbinsel im Hoch- und Spätmittelalter,* ed. Matthias M. Tischler and Alexander Fidora (Münster: Aschendorff, 2011), 445–68.

his army at Las Navas and, according to Rodrigo, men "from nearly all of Europe" joined him for the fight. Alongside Spanish noblemen, the author mentioned French and Italians from beyond the mountains. Before the battle took place, however, these "foreigners" (*gens alienigena*) took flight, leaving the Spanish to fight alone (*Historia de Rebus Hispaniae*, bk. 8, chap. 4; *BE* 236). Instead of presenting a "European" Christian army, as the *Mozarabic Chronicle from 754* had done, Rodrigo seized the opportunity to highlight the special role played by the Spanish in their fight against the Muslim "invaders."

Several decades later, this motif was picked up in the vernacular *Primera crónica general de España*, and a number of texts from Spain and elsewhere explained that the Almohad Caliph Muhammad al-Nasir (d. 1213) tried to invade Spain in order to ultimately conquer all of Europe (an idea that is also alluded to in a charter granted by Alfonso VIII to Rodrigo Jiménez in 1213). So, successful military resistance became a Spanish exploit (*BE* 256). This is all the more revealing since the vernacular historiographic tradition in Spain expresses a clear consciousness of the peninsula's position on the margins of Europe, all the while insisting upon its being part of the continent. The Mediterranean separated Europe and Africa, but another—perhaps more important—border separated the "land of the Christians" (*tierra de los cristianos*) and the "land of the Moors" (*tierra de [los] moros*) (*BE* 259). This border was inside Spain and made the continental divide a secondary consideration. In a quite complex and asymmetric constellation, Spanish vernacular historiographic texts tend to identify "Africa" as the place of origin of the "Moors," who came into Spain where the Christian inhabitants of this country fought them. Although the peninsula was often clearly identified as a part of Europe, the fight against the Muslim became a primarily Spanish affair (at least until the end of the fifteenth century, when Europe became more widely used, for instance in the works of Alfonso de Palencia).[6]

---

**6** For this paragraph, see Oschema, *Bilder von Europa*, 256–62.

In both contexts, the period of the early crusades as well as the "Reconquista," the idea of an exterior menace was at least partly misleading: from the eleventh century onwards, the Christian rulers on the Iberian Peninsula continually expanded their rule, and when pope Urban II tried to motivate Christian believers to help their fellow Christians in the East, the Seljuk advances in Anatolia had given way to power-struggles amongst the Muslim realms in the Levant. Still the motif worked to motivate the recipients of the above-mentioned texts to expansive behaviour and action. The situation was different in Eastern Europe during the early thirteenth century when faced by Mongol expansion after different tribes had been successfully united by Temüdschin—the famous Genghis Khan. Having conquered large swaths of land between their central Asian origin and China, their military campaigns then led them to Eastern Europe around 1220. News of the unfamiliar conquerors from the East and their fierce and violent practices travelled fast and led to the proliferation of images of inhuman brutality and numerous stereotypes.[7]

The experience of populations under attack was doubtless cruel and traumatizing, and the situation was perceived as an external menace that led, once again, to an increased use of European motifs. For instance, in a letter to Pope Innocent IV (1243–1254), sent either in 1250 or 1254, King Bela IV of Hungary (1235–1270) complained bitterly about his fellow "Christian princes of Europe." While the "Tartars" menaced the borders of his realm, none of these Christian rulers had effectively come to his aid, even though, according to Bela, the fall of his kingdom would incur greater dangers for the "inhabitants of Europe" (*Europe habitatoribus*) (*BE* 294) than the fall of Constantinople or even of the Holy Land. He thus implored the pontiff to appeal to the other rulers for help,

---

**7** On the Mongol expansion, see Peter Jackson, *The Mongols and the West, 1221–1410* (Harlow: Pearson Longman, 2005); concerning questions of mutual perception, see Antti Ruotsala, *Europeans and Mongols in the Middle of the Thirteenth Century. Encountering the Other* (Helsinki: Finnish Academy of Science and Letters, 2001).

proposing the construction of a line of defence on the Danube that would secure his realm's well-being and that of Europe.

Bela's choice of words is noteworthy, but not entirely without precedent. In a letter from July 3, 1241 to King Henry III of England (1216–1272), known to us only through Matthew Paris's *Chronicle*, Emperor Frederick II (1215–1250) also described the attacks of the new adversaries and invited the English king to join the fight. While Frederick explained that the Mongols were attacking Christians (*christianitas*, *respublica Christi*) and sought to dominate the Occident, his call to joint resistance conjured up the image of a victorious "imperial Europe" (*BE* 295).

Contemporary historiographers also seized upon the well-established motif that news about these attacks had spread across Europe (and "even the climes of the Saracen," as Matthew Paris put it), but many authors did not necessarily perceive the conflict in these terms. In fact, the absence of Europe in historiographical works produced in close time and space to the events in Hungary is quite remarkable: Thomas of Split, for example, noted the appearance of a comet in 1239 over the kingdom of Hungary and that earlier in the year a solar eclipse had been visible "in all of Europe" (*BE* 297–98). His detailed descriptions of the Mongols' attacks, on the other hand, do not categorize the conflict in continental terms. The context of the "Mongol threat" is thus an ambivalent case: while a number of diplomatic texts did refer to the menace to the border and inhabitants of Europe—a circular letter from 1260 in which Pope Alexander IV addressed secular and ecclesiastical princes emphasized the Mongols' desire to enter Europe and then conquer the entire world—the historiographers seemed to have been rather reluctant to do so, especially when they were close to the events.

The most prominent case of external threat helped the further development and use of the notion of Europe: namely, the expansion of Ottoman rule and its shocking high-point with the conquest of Constantinople in 1453.[8] From the four-

---

**8** For a general overview, see Halil İnalcık, *The Ottoman Empire, 1300–1600* (London: Phoenix, 2000).

teenth century, Ottoman rulers had successfully expanded their dominions and quickly established themselves permanently in regions west of the Bosporus. It was not before the end of the century that they started to be perceived more clearly by Latin Christianity as a major threat. An important moment was doubtless the battle of Nicopolis in 1396, when a composite army of French, Venetian, German, and Hungarian contingents under the command of King Sigismund of Hungary (the later emperor) suffered a bloody defeat at the hands of Sultan Bayezid I.[9] The event's importance is reflected, among numerous other texts, in the works of the widely travelled French moralist, politician, and clergyman Philippe de Mézières:[10] Philippe was a constant propagator of a new crusade and had long tried to motivate Christian rulers to take up the fight against the Muslims. In his famous *Songe du viel pelerin* (ca. 1389), Europe does not yet play a particularly prominent role: the name appears, amongst others, in a description of the tripartite structure of the world and in a list of regions that had allegedly been dominated by the "French" kings of the distant past. Even in his *Letter to King Richard II* from 1395, Philippe focused on the well-being of Christendom and addressed the "Christians of the Occident." Shortly after Nicopolis, however, his tone changed. In the *Epistre lamentable*, Philippe addressed Duke Philip the Bold of Burgundy, one of the most powerful figures in France, whose son John (the Fearless) had been captured in the battle: the *Epistre*

---

**9** Aziz Atiya, *The Crusade of Nicopolis* (London: Methuen, 1934), remains classical; for more recent approaches, see *Nicopolis, 1396–1996*, ed. Jacques Paviot (Dijon: Société des Annales de Bourgogne, 1997).

**10** For the following paragraph, see Klaus Oschema, "De l'universalisme périmé au refuge de la chrétienté: l'Europe de Philippe de Mézières," in *Philippe de Mézières et l'Europe: Nouvelle histoire, nouveaux espaces, nouveaux langages*, ed. Joël Blanchard and Renate Blumenfeld-Kosinski (Geneva: Droz, 2017), 27–50; more generally on Philippe de Mézières, see *Philippe de Mézières and his Age: Piety and Politics in the Fourteenth Century*, ed. Renate Blumenfeld-Kosinski and Kiril Petkov (Leiden: Brill, 2012).

deplored the fatal blow the Christians in Europe had suffered and underscored that the Turks had already conquered large parts of Christian lands, "especially in Europe." Since Philippe feared that the "infidel" wanted to conquer the rest of the continent, he called for a new crusade to recover the lost parts of Europe—and after that, Armenia and Syria.

A few years later, though, Sultan Bayezid suffered a major defeat at the hands of the Mongol ruler Tamerlane in the battle of Ankara (1402). His death in captivity (1403)—which stalled the Ottoman advance towards the West. In the long run, however, the motif of the "Turkish menace" to Europe did not disappear: not only did humanists write about the ongoing conflicts in the East in European terms, but Europe also found its way into the language of diplomacy. When he repeated the prohibition of trade with the "infidel" in 1422, Pope Martin V explicitly referred to the "Turks who moved from Asia into Europe" (*BE* 286). From the 1430s onwards, this use of the word became increasingly prominent: when he congratulated the Holy Roman king Albert III on his election in 1438, for example, Pope Eugene IV expressed his hope that the new monarch would protect the Church and "dispel the infidel from Europe" (*BE* 287). In the same year, a letter by King Ladislas of Poland to Pope Eugene used similar wording.

Why this notion of the defence of Europe and its borders rapidly became common currency is not entirely clear. It may have had to do with early humanists' aesthetic appreciation for the "classical" ring of the continent's name; another important factor might have been refugees of Greek origin, who fled Byzantine lands in growing numbers and brought their books and knowledge with them. This movement was furthered by the council of Ferrara and Florence in 1438, where clerics from the Roman Church met an important Greek delegation to discuss the union of both churches. One of the Greek delegates was the monk Bessarion (1399/1408–1472), who chose to stay in the West where he became a cardinal. In a letter to the later Emperor Constantine IX Palaeologus (1404–1453), written between 1443 and 1446, Bessarion praised the addressee as the future liberator of Europe... (*BE* 287)

The scene was thus well-set for the famous speech *Constantinopolitana clades* by Enea Silvio Piccolomini (later Pope Pius II, 1458–1464) at the imperial diet at Frankfurt in 1454.[11] The princes of the empire had assembled to discuss how to respond to the Ottoman conquest of Constantinople that had so shocked Latin Christendom. In his function as imperial secretary and delegate, Enea Silvio was a determined propagator of a new crusade, and his speech presented dramatic images.[12] The ideas he developed for his audience strongly resembled older models, including William of Malmesbury's version of Urban II's sermon. But Enea Silvio went much further when he depicted Europe as a homeland (*patria*) of the Christians, who were being menaced in their own house (*domus propria*) after the fall of Constantinople. Despite everything that had long separated the Latin and the Greek churches, Enea Silvio did not hesitate to appeal to his listeners by depicting Constantinople as the "second eye" and the "second hand" of Christendom that had been severed from the body (*BE* 302).

This speech at Frankfurt was not the first time that Enea Silvio referred to Europe and the need to defend it in the context of the conflicts with the Ottomans: references to Europe already abound in his letters from the 1440s, and earlier in 1454 he had emphasized the Ottomans' movement towards Europe at another imperial diet at Regensburg. On that occa-

---

11 See Helmrath, "Pius II. und die Türken," 93–94; for the text, see *Deutsche Reichstagsakten unter Kaiser Friedrich III.*, vol. 5, no. 2: *Reichsversammlung zu Frankfurt 1454*, ed. Johannes Helmrath and Gabriele Annas (Munich: Oldenbourg, 2013), 463–565. An English translation by Michael von Cotta-Schönberg is available online: https://hal.archives-ouvertes.fr/hal-01097147/document (accessed July 25, 2022).

12 On Enea Silvio's life, see Volker Reinhardt, *Pius II. Piccolomini: Der Papst, mit dem die Renaissance begann* (Munich: Beck, 2013); cf. Nancy Bisaha, "'Inventing Europe' with Aeneas Silvius Piccolomini," in *Images of Otherness in Medieval and Early Modern Times*, ed. Anja Eisenbeiß and Lieselotte Saurma-Jeltsch (Berlin: Deutscher Kunstverlag, 2012), 143–50.

sion, the participants had even agreed to gather an army large enough to "expel" the Turks "from Europe"—it is quite probable that Enea Silvio himself drafted this text (*BE* 303).

From this moment on, references to Europe as the homeland of Christians and one that had to be protected against exterior incursions or freed from external conquerors—Muslims—became relatively common. But although such references appeared even in diplomatic contexts (the plan to "expel" the Turks "from Europe" is mentioned repeatedly in the correspondence of King Matthew Corvinus from Hungary), they were never as numerous and prominent as the references to Christendom and Christianity. As for Enea Silvio, he continued to use the phrase: after his election as Pope Pius II in 1456, he tried to organize a new crusade and in the crusade bull *Ezechielis prophete* from October 22, 1463, he explicitly asked God to grant the Christians victory against "his" enemies, so that they might praise him "in all of Europe...."[13] It is important to note that Pius did not finish the sentence here: in conformity with the universal outlook of the Roman Church, he added "and that the entire world may adore you and sing thy name forever." This detail is significant since it signals that although Europe and (Latin) Christendom had at that point converged and that the Latin Church and its followers felt menaced from outside, the two notions were not synonymous (as can sometimes be read in older discussions of this topic)—and neither did the Church limit its aspirations to one continent.

## "Nostrifying" Europe— Identities and Identifications

Enea Silvio Piccolomini traditionally occupies an important place in studies on the use of the concept of Europe in the Middle Ages—and rightfully so. At the same time, we need

---

**13** Oschema, "L'idée d'Europe," 79; the text of *Ezechielis prophete* is edited in Guillaume Fillastre d. J., *Ausgewählte Werke*, ed. Malte Prietzel (Ostfildern: Thorbecke, 2003), 158–205 at 166 and 204.

to situate his work in a broader context to understand his practices and his role properly. More than once, his use of the name of the continent seems to express a strong identification with Europe, which he describes as the homeland of Christendom, especially for the Latin Christians who followed the doctrines of the Roman Church. While Enea Silvio's speech from 1454 underscores solidarity with Greek Christians, other texts demonstrate that he was still critical towards the East. This becomes clear, for example, in a curious text probably written in 1461, when Enea Silvio had already become Pope Pius II. The work's intended readership is hard to gauge: in purely formal terms, the *Epistola ad Mahumetem* pretends to be a letter to Sultan Mehmet II, whom Pius beseeches to accept the Christian faith so that he might become a worthy ruler for his large dominions.[14] Should he not accept the "true religion," the pontiff explains, Mehmet would never acquire any renown amongst the "Europeans and the peoples of the Occident" (*Europaeos et Occidentales populos*) (*BE* 305). Pius II continues that until that moment Mehmet had only dealt with Christians who were basically "heretics" (Armenians, Jacobites, Maronites, but most importantly the Greeks) and that he only ever ruled over a limited number of Christians. Should he continue his expansion towards the West, however, he would be confronted with "true" believers in the Occident, where the Italians, Spaniards, Hungarians, and French would resolutely resist him.

The *Epistola ad Mahumetem* is hard to interpret, and we neither know whether it was ever sent to Mehmet nor if it was ever even intended for the sultan's eyes. More than forty manuscripts and several early prints of the text survive, and it is quite plausible that Pius wrote it first and foremost to motivate Catholic Christians by fostering their hope of successful resistance. In this case, it might express a new interpretation of the "*angulus*-motif": Christendom still appears as having

---

**14** Enea Silvio Piccolomini/Pius II, *Epistola ad Mahumetem. Einleitung, kritische Edition, Übersetzung*, ed. Reinhold F. Glei and Markus Köhler (Trier: Wissenschaftlicher Verlag Trier, 2001).

been reduced to Europe (or just a part of it), but there was hope, since the number of Christians outside the continent was limited and their faith not "true"—in contrast to "European" Christians. In its vocabulary, the text also furnishes a good example for the use of a collective noun, since Pius explicitly mentions the *Europaeos*—something he had already done in his *Gesta sub Federico III* (also known as *De Europa*) (*BE* 306). As a result Enea Silvio has often been credited with the (re-)invention of a word that had not been used since the mid-eighth century (in the *Mozarabic Chronicle of 754*).

A closer look reveals, however, that he was not the only author in his day to use such a term. It is true that several earlier authors had difficulties finding an adequate word: Dante, for example, in his *De Monarchia* quite awkwardly contrasted the "people who inhabit Europe" (*Europam colentes*) (bk. 3, chap. 14, §7) with the Asians and the Africans, for whom he had no trouble using the collective noun. In other works, we find an adjective, "Europicus," that never became well-established: the *Annales Xantenses* (ninth century) mentioned the *Europico ponto*, the *Gesta Sancti Servatii* (twelfth century) situated the Brabant town of Tongeren in the centre of the "European world" (*Europico orbis*). Even Boccaccio in the fourteenth century was still grappling with this problem in his commentary to Dante's *Divina Commedia*, where he distinguished the African sea from the "European" (*Europico*) one. Some have argued that this form might have been inspired by Greek influence. Meanwhile, Joannes Balbus's *Catholicon* dictionary (thirteenth century) mentioned the more Latinate forms *europius* and *europia*, which also found few followers.[15]

While similar coinages appear from time to time, the mid-fifteenth century clearly constituted a crucial phase—and Enea Silvio was neither the only author who started speaking of the "Europeans" at this time, nor the first: between 1453 and 1455, for example, the humanist Lampo Birago who was active at the Roman curia, distinguished in his *Strategicon*

---

**15** For this paragraph, see Oschema, *Bilder von Europa*, 441.

*adversus Turcos* between the Europeans (*Europaeos*) and the Asians (*BE* 442–43). Like Enea Silvio, he might have been influenced by the predilections of humanists as well as by Greek usage. In any case, the term seems to have rapidly become quite common: even in relatively pragmatic texts, such as annual prognostications (*Judicia anni*), references to the "European Christians" (*christiani europiani*) and the like can be found from the 1470s onwards (*BE* 425). So, by the end of the fifteenth century, a collective noun "Europeans" as well as an accompanying adjective were both widely accepted and used.

This linguistic innovation was intimately connected with political, social, and cultural developments of this period, but it also built on earlier phenomena, from the twelfth century, that expressed the growing identification of Latin authors with Europe—a process that might be described as "nostrification" in the sense that these authors increasingly tended to refer to Europe as "our" (i.e., "their") part of the world.

The first explicit references of such a claim date to the twelfth century and mostly contain indirect identifications: we have already seen that Urban II allegedly presented Europe, according to William of Malmesbury, as the part of the world that "we Christians inhabit." At about the same time, Honorius Augustodunensis had a more universal perspective in mind: when he mentioned the part of the world that "we inhabit" (*a nobis incolitur*), he referred to the entire known *ecumene* (*BE* 433). A few decades later, however, Gottfried of Viterbo described Europe again as being inhabited by Christians (he avoided the first person in his text and thus did not explicitly identify himself with them, though it's hardly conceivable that he wanted to exclude himself). Since several texts from the twelfth and thirteenth centuries acknowledged the presence of non-Christians in Europe, perhaps a clear-cut identification was neither opportune nor conceivable. On the other hand, we cannot always expect our authors to develop entirely coherent images: in the early fourteenth century, for example, the anonymous author of the *Directorium ad passagium faciendum* did mention the presence of the "infidel" in Europe, but this did not preclude him from calling the continent "our part [of the world]" only a few lines later (*BE* 283). In any case, our interpretation of this and other texts must account for the fact that their authors were aiming to motivate their readers in highly polemic contexts. This is, of course, equally true for the later texts by Enea Silvio: in many cases, he did not seek to present a factual description of his world, but rather to provide a "weaponized" version of things to pressure his audience into taking action.

Against this backdrop, it is highly instructive to look at some more sober texts from this period, ones that primarily sought to convey knowledge, such as philosophical treatises or encyclopaedias. Although they tend to refer to Europe much more succinctly, these texts equally confirm the slow but steady construction of the motif of "our Europe." Vincent of Beauvais, for example, matter-of-factly spoke of "our summer in Europe" or identified and described things "here in Europe" (with an undertone of "at our place"). An anonymous commentator of Pseudo-Bede's *De mundi celestis terrestrisque constititutione* working at the monastery of Tegernsee in the twelfth century, had already stated: "Europe is our region..." (*Europa est nostra regio*) (*BE* 435). In many cases, these passages focused on a broad range of phenomena that they merely wanted to situate geographically. Over time, such formulations slowly contributed to a process of self-identification with Europe that became increasingly perceptible. So it is little surprise that Konrad of Megenberg, who wrote his *Book of Nature* around 1350, not only gave a short description of where Europe was to be found but also concluded rather nonchalantly: "And we are in this part" (*In dem selben teil sei wir*) (bk. 2, chap. 32).

That these brief moments of self-identification were not confined to an intellectual elite of clerics and the erudite, can conveniently be demonstrated with the example of one of the most successful literary texts of the Late Middle Ages: the *Travels* of John of Mandeville (the author's identity is still a matter of debate). Compiled in Northern France in the 1350s, the work soon became a bestseller: around three hundred manuscripts, seventy-two printed editions from the fifteenth and sixteenth centuries, and translations into more than ten languages are known.[16] Even though the text does not describe a real journey, but is the compilation of an armchair traveller, it is of extraordinary value for our reconstruction of concepts and ideas about the world that were widely held by people in late medieval Europe. The most pertinent passage on Europe can be found in a short comment on the descendants of Noah, which repeats the idea that Japheth's sons effectively peopled Europe: *and of Japheth [came] the folk of Israel and we that dwell in Europe*. Although late medieval travelogues rarely use European terminology, Mandeville concurs here with John of Marignola, who had equally referred to "Europe, where we are."[17]

From the fourteenth century onwards, analogous passages became widespread: the French cleric and scholar Nicole Oresme underlined that "we are in Europe," and in the late fifteenth century, the Swiss humanist monk Albrecht of Bonstetten included a quite elaborate geographical introduction in his *Description of the Swiss Confederation* (1479), which presented the territories of the Confederation as occupying the heart of Europe. Seeking to further the acceptance of the Confederation amongst the neighbouring monarchs, Bonstetten addressed a series of lavishly illustrated manuscripts of his work to King Louis XI of France, Pope Sixtus IV, and others. The extant exemplars contain a series of cartographic images that evoke a zooming-in effect: starting with the cosmological depiction of Atlas, two *mappaemundi* followed, in the second of which Europe received particular attention. The last image in the series focused on the Confederation, whose lands are shown to be organized around the mountain Rigi (near Lucerne and Schwyz). The text itself does not argue

---

**16** *Jean de Mandeville: Le livre des merveilles du monde*, ed. Christiane Deluz (Paris: CNRS, 2000); *Jean de Mandeville in Europa: neue Perspektiven in der Reiseliteraturforschung*, ed. Ernst Bremer (Paderborn: Fink, 2007).

**17** For this and the following paragraph, see Oschema, *Bilder von Europa*, 435–39.

any further with specific characteristics of "Europeanness," but Bonstetten's work demonstrates the degree to which the idea of situating oneself in the continent had become established by his time. In addition, it offers a convincing example in which the use of this geographical frame is not explicitly based on the othering of Asia and Africa, but rather on the perspective from inside Europe.

In this respect, Bonstetten built upon older models: amongst the authors who reflected on the "nature" of Europe, the German cleric Alexander of Roes certainly occupies a special place. Writing in the 1280s, in his *Noticia Saeculi* he focused consciously on Europe, its order, and its condition. Alexander declared that he would leave the description of Asia and Africa and their inhabitants to others, since his concern was Europe and the Christians, which he saw as closely connected.[18] The intricate combination of geographical, chronological, and cultural elements (including politics and religion) in his text expresses the difficulties that arise from the tension between a primarily geographical definition of Europe and the attempt to approach it as a cultural unity. For Alexander, Europe consisted of four major kingdoms, which he arranged according to the points of the compass: Greece in the East, Spain in the West, the "Roman kingdom" in the South, and the "Kingdom of the Franks" in the North (*BE* 372). This was not the first attempt to identify a limited number of "important" kingdoms in Europe: the *Vita Regiswindis*, for example, written in the twelfth century, attributed to Emperor Louis the Pious the rule over Italy, France, and Germany, which the author identified as the "foremost" or "outstanding" (*praestantiores*) realms of Europe (*BE* 376).

But Alexander went considerably further. While he unambiguously included Greece in Europe in his first list, he immediately attributed a special role to the Romans and the Franks, whose kingdoms he described not only as major

---

**18** Alexander's works are edited in Alexander von Roes, *Schriften*, ed. Herbert Grundmann and Hermann Heimpel (Stuttgart: Hiersemann, 1958); cf. Fuhrmann, "Alexander von Roes".

(*principalis*), but "more major" (*principalior*). Focusing on the latter regions, he developed an intricate tripartite model, in which he attributed specific functions (as a result of a historical process) to France, Italy, and Germany. As a cleric, he considered the Christian faith to represent the apogee of humanity; in his own day, he declared, "the Roman Church reside[d] in Europe" (*res publica ecclesie Romane residet in Europa*) (*BE* 373)—more precisely in Italy. Italy and Rome had thus inherited the function of priesthood (*sacerdotium*), while the other parts of the "most principal" kingdoms shared the functions of study (*studium*), which belonged to France (*Gallia*), and of political rulership (*imperium*), which the German kingdom (*Teutonia*) had inherited. Alexander then enumerated the positive, neutral, and negative character traits of the Italians, the French, and the Germans, and discussed further aspects of the politics of his time. But the most important element of his work for our purposes is the idea that Europe was not just a geographical unit but also a cultural one that had developed historically and that possessed a political and cultural order. While Greece belonged to Europe in a geographical sense, it did not merit any particular mention as far as functional organization goes. The four main realms of Europe— Greece, Italy (or rather the Empire, combining Germany and Northern Italy), France, and Spain—are still identified as such in the fifteenth century, for instance in the Spanish *Libro de las generaciones* or in Pierre d'Ailly's *Imago mundi*.

The far-reaching approximation of Europe and the Church in Alexander's work is remarkable, especially since other authors of his time explicitly underlined Europe's quasi "eccentric" position. In the 1270s, Humbert of Romans, the master general of the Dominican order, produced a treatise to justify a new crusade against the "Saracens." The argument in his *Opus tripartitum* was partly historical, explaining that Christians had once ruled large parts of Asia and Africa, from which they had then been expelled by the "infidel conquerors"—only parts of Europe had remained (a motif with which we are already familiar) (*BE* 277-78). As a result, Humbert accepted that in his day Europe had become the home of

Christendom, at least for the moment: in his *De predicatione crucis*, written ca. 1266–1288, he explicitly called Europe the "[part] where we are" (*in qua nos sumus*) (*BE* 279). Nevertheless, he underlined the religious inferiority of this part in comparison with the Holy Land, where Christ had been born.

The examples in this section have shown an important development and the tensions or problems it created: on the one hand, authors in the Latin West increasingly identified with the part of the world they inhabited. They either situated themselves *in* Europe or even went so far as to call Europe plainly "our" (i.e., their) part of the world. On the other hand, this did not mean that in their imagination Europe and Christendom were one and the same. Quite the contrary: attempts to describe and explain how Europe had come to be the part of the world where Christians lived, express a sense of historical development. A situation that might, at best, be grudgingly accepted as a transient state that invited the believers to prepare for a "better" future in which Christianity would—once again—rule over the entire world. Seen from this perspective, "Christian Europe" (a formula that does not appear in these texts) could hardly be more than a temporary phenomenon in their eyes—a perspective that coincided with the perception of the material world as an exile for any "true" Christian.

## Becoming Superior? Europe in the Perception of Late Medieval Authors

So Europe not only became a frame of reference for late medieval authors, it also became an increasingly "nostrified" geographical unit. But did these authors develop specific and more far-reaching ideas about "their" part of the world? We have already seen initial traces. First, the notion of Europe being used when menaced from beyond (whether the menace was real or imaginary), leading to a widespread tendency to "Christianize" Europe in the sense of describing it as the continent where Christians lived. But Europe did not automatically acquire a deeper religious meaning. In fact, attempts to imbue the continent with such connotations (starting with

Sulpicius Severus's comments on St. Martin of Tours) reveal the difficulties of such an endeavour. Claiming a specifically religious signification for Europe necessitated convoluted exegesis. Second, the distribution of different cultural functions amongst the major kingdoms—i.e., Italy, France, and Germany—as proposed by Alexander of Roes represents a conscious and elaborate attempt to ascribe a specific character and order to Europe. However, Alexander's ideas on this specific problem (he also discusses the political order of the Empire, the Emperors' privileges etc.) do not appear to have found any immediate followers. Thus, the question remains whether contemporary and later authors ascribed specific characteristics to Europe—and if so, what were they?

In most cases such attempts were selective and unsystematic: quite often they merely prolonged the established practice of using Europe as frame of reference. A number of texts presented Italy as the noblest region of the continent, and they certainly implied a hierarchy but this was rarely made more explicit. In the fourteenth century, such passages can be found in the *Eulogium historiarum*, a mid-fourteenth century chronicle from Malmesbury Abbey, as well as in Dante's *De Monarchia*. Probably motivated by "patriotism," others claimed preeminence for their own regions of origin: hence Robert Mannyng probably meant England and Ireland, when he declared "these are the best" in his *Chronicle* in the 1330s (*BE* 325), and Pierre d'Ailly argued in the early fifteenth century that France was the largest kingdom in Europe in his day (he did concede, however, that Italy was the "most beautiful") (*BE* 326).

Another, more precise category that served as a basis for comparisons, this time between Europe and the other parts of the world, concerned population size and settlement. From the thirteenth century onwards, several authors underlined the former, arguing that the number of inhabitants in Europe would ensure its victory in conflicts with armies from Asia or Africa. Gervase of Tilbury introduced this idea in passing, and later authors developed it more systematically, sometimes adding comments on the quality of the population. In the mid-fourteenth century, Ranulph Higden seized on the theory of climates to justify Europe's superior position in comparison with Africa: while the intensity of the sun supposedly caused Africans to be small, dark-skinned, and curly haired (according to him), the people of Europe were supposedly larger, stronger, braver, and more beautiful (*BE* 327). Considering population size and the number of settlements, John of Sultaniya explained in his *Libellus de notitia orbis* (ca. 1402) that Europe was much more densely populated than Asia (*BE* 327).

Apart from these rather unsystematic and scattered asides, two main currents of thinking about Europe and its character can be identified. The first of these was mainly inspired by religious motifs and approaches, even though they entailed ideas about political and administrative order. The second primarily relied on classical ideas about the climates and their effects. In many cases, the resulting observations and arguments intersect, but it is best to discuss them separately.

From the perspective of a mainly religious discourse, a specific position of Europe could be claimed in different ways: one was to simply refer, in a quasi-empirical way, to the presence of saints, their number, and their importance. In so doing, one could claim a religious status for the continent that had accrued through historical process, without any further, more deep-reaching justification. A second approach, which developed early on and became increasingly prominent towards the late Middle Ages, consisted in the aforementioned references to the biblical story of the distribution of lands amongst Noah's sons (and consequently, their descendants). Once Shem, Ham, and Japheth were identified with the three parts of the world in the Early Middle Ages, the story of Genesis 9 furnished additional material for further interpretation: Shem (inheriting Asia) had been blessed by his father, while Ham (i.e., Africa) had been cursed. Japheth's position was somewhat ambivalent: while the chosen people of Israel was usually connected to Shem, Japheth's descendants were largely identified as the pagan peoples, the *gentes*, who lived in Europe.[19] Since Christianity had effected their conversion, however, this originally marginal position could acquire more positive connotations: Gen. 9:20–25 predicted that the sons of Japheth should receive ample space and dwell in the tents of Shem. To many Latin Christian authors this meant that the *gentes* were chosen to ultimately lead the Church, while Ham was predestined to become the serf of his brothers.

These ideas furnished a basis for a non-neutral perception of a Europe that had become largely Christianized by the eleventh century; they also provided the grounds for more far-reaching interpretations. Adding to the exegetical tradition, Honorius Augustodunensis highlighted the social dimension when he explained in his *Imago mundi* that the descendants of Shem were the ancestors of free men (*liberos*), those of Japheth warriors (*milites*), and those of Ham serfs (*servi*) (bk. 3, chap. 1). This interpretation must have been hard to reconcile with the social realities of medieval Europe: even if the idealizing model of a tripartite society (that usually distinguished clergy, warriors/noblemen, and labourers) became widespread from the eleventh century onwards, Honorius's model could hardly explain the presence of free men and serfs in Europe. In spite of this apparent problem, however, Europe might in fact have been perceived by some as a home of warriors: a twelfth-century candlestick, probably from the region of Lièges and today part of the treasure of Hildesheim cathedral provides the only surviving explicit personification of the continents from the Middle Ages.[20] The artist, who is only known as the "Master of Stavelot," identified each of the three female figures that sit on the candlestick's base with a segment of a *mappamundi* representing the respective part of the world that they hold in their left hands. Each of these segments is inscribed with the continent's name. In their right hand, every figure holds a symbolic object that equally carries an inscription: Asia holds a vessel inscribed *DIVITIE* ("riches"), Africa an open book with the inscription *SAPIENTIA*

---

**19** See already Fischer, *Oriens*, 10–19.

**20** See Oschema, *Bilder von Europa*, 499–501 and fig. 34.

("knowledge"), and Europa a shield inscribed *BELLUM* ("war") and a sword. As Odile Wattel-de Croizant has pointed out, this figure might represent the motif of a *Europa promachos*, a "warrior Europe," descending from ancient Greek tradition. At the same time, the concordance with Honorius's model is also striking, at least as far as Europe is concerned.

The idea that the distribution of lands between Noah's sons was also the moment when a tripartite social order was established seems not to have become particularly wide-spread—in contrast to the numerous genealogical tables that tried to identify the peoples of the medieval world with the seventy-two peoples that appear in Genesis 10. But there are traces of a certain medieval afterlife: in his famous *Sachsen-spiegel*, a record of laws and customs that he compiled ca. 1220/1235 and that soon came to be perceived as having normative value, Eike von Repgow mentioned the episode. He underscored that Ham had not been blessed—but he drew no further consequences. On the contrary, he explicitly argued against those who believed that serfdom resulted from Ham's curse: according to Eike, the real reason for serfdom was "force, imprisonment, and unjustified violence" (*van dwange unde van venknisse unde van unrechter gewalt*) (*Landrecht* III.42,6). Even though he explicitly declared Japheth to be "our ancestor" (*unse vordere*) (*Landrecht* III.42,3), he clearly had difficulties imagining further cultural and social effects deriving from such a genealogy.

While Eike's text furnished a kind of negative proof—he is arguing against a position that must have been in circulation—texts that explicitly express such an idea remain rare. One example is the so-called *Österreichische Chronik von den 95 Herrschaften*, compiled by an anonymous author in the late fourteenth century. Here Shem appears as the ancestor of the free, Ham and Africa are identified with the origin of the serfs, and Japheth in Europe is presented as the forefather of the noblemen (MGH Dt. Chron. 6, bk. 1, §15). Despite the scarcity of such explicit presentations, we should not underestimate the effects of the more general identification of the parts of the world with Noah's descendants or the complementary stories about the Trojan origin of numerous peoples who inhabited late medieval Europe.

Keeping this in mind is particularly important since late medieval authors did occasionally reflect quite explicitly upon cultural characteristics that they explained with analogous arguments: according to Dante, for example, several large linguistic groups were created after the destruction of the tower of Babel (*De vulgari eloquentia*, 1303–1305). Three of these had migrated into Europe: one settled in the South and another one in the North, while the Greek lived partly in Europe and partly in Asia. After the migration, these linguistic groups became increasingly differentiated, but their relations remained identifiable, as did their customs (*mores*) and appearance (*habitus*). Observations of this kind were not entirely new: Brunetto Latini (d. 1294), for example, had already described the pronunciation of the languages of the Orient as "guttural," those in the centre of the *ecumene* as "palatal," and those in the Occident as "dental" (*BE* 343).

The identification of the inhabitants of Europe with the descendants of Japheth can also be confirmed by a kind of control test, since genealogies for European peoples that refer to Ham or Shem rather than Japheth are rare.[21] According to John of Marignola (d. ca. 1359) and his *Chronica Boemorum* some believed that the Slavic and Bohemian peoples were actually descendants of Ham, though he explicitly refutes this idea. John might have been reacting to texts like the anonymous *Chronicon imperatorum et Pontificum Bavaricum* (thirteenth century), which in effect described the Slavs and the Ruthenians as the "sons of Ham" (and curiously declared the Slavs to be *Mauritani*). But this text was written from an external perspective and probably sought to denigrate the peoples in question by excluding them from the common Japhetite ancestry. That such descendance would have been perceived as problematic can be seen in the *Historia Brittonum*, usually ascribed to Nennius: according to this text, the Britons descended from Ham via their ancestor Brutus. Once

---

21 See for this paragraph Oschema, *Bilder von Europa*, 345–48.

again, this presentation might have been the result of a process of othering since the text was likely written in Wales. In any case, it was not very successful. While a Hamite ancestry clearly had negative connotations, a Semite origin might have evoked a more positive resonance: in the early tenth century, for example, Asser presented his protagonist King Alfred as a descendant of Shem, and several later authors picked this up (Aelred of Rievaulx, Symeon of Durham, Matthew Paris). Nevertheless, this genealogical construct remained marginal: overall, late medieval authors clearly perceived Europe to be inhabited by the descendants of Japheth.

Another prominent image that drew on biblical traditions and connected them with the tripartite structure of the *orbis* was the motif of the three magi, who were interpreted as representing the three parts of the world that embraced Christian belief and thus symbolized the universal character of the Church. In order to develop this image, quite a lot of exegetical work had to be done: the magi only appear very briefly in the gospel of St. Matthew (Matt. 2:1–12), which mentions neither their actual number nor their names. First traces of the number three appear from the third century onwards, but this did not become more widespread before the seventh and eighth centuries, and interpretations continued to vary. As to the names, the so-called *Excerpta latini Barbari*, a short chronicle originally written in Greek around 500 and translated into a rather crude Latin around 700, mentioned them as *Bithisarea*, *Melichior*, and *Gathaspa* (*BE* 492)—which later became Caspar, Melchior, and Balthasar. The identification of these three—who were soon depicted as kings and frequently represented in medieval art—with the three parts of the world became well-established from the ninth century onwards, for instance in a work attributed to pseudo-Bede and nowadays interpreted as an abridged version of Hrabanus Maurus's *Commentary on the Gospel of St. Matthew*. What remained unclear, however, was the question of which magus (or "king") represented which part of the world and how their connection could be constructed? The earliest exegetes were not overly concerned about this—Otfried of Weissenburg (d.

ca. 870), for instance, explicitly declared that the three magi "mystically" stood for the three parts of the world (*BE* 492). He would probably have considered an attempt to construct a specific identification to be misleading. Later authors argued less subtly. Even a thinker like Anselm of Laon (d. 1117) declared that the magi were three because they came from the *gentes* of the three parts of the world (*tres sunt, qui de tribus partibus mundi gentes veniunt*) (*BE* 493).

Towards the end of the Middle Ages, this kind of explicit identification became more prevalent, as is mirrored in pictorial representations: the magi represented different kinds of triads, including three different ages which were expressed by their depiction as young, middle-aged, and old. In addition, from the thirteenth century onwards texts and images mainly from the German and neighbouring regions started to distinguish not only the age and the different gifts of the magi, they also began to represent one of them, often the youngest, Caspar, with darker skin and physiological traits that they identified with Africa. Even late-medieval heraldic collections that showed the magi's coats of arms (which were obviously invented, since heraldry was a twelfth-century innovation) seem to have distinguished a "dark-skinned" magus from a "semitic" type and a more "European" one, as Michael Wintle has observed. Wintle concludes that this tradition was a fundamental stepping-stone in the "blackening" of Africa in the late medieval imaginary.[22] However, our sources are not always entirely clear, since the attribution of the heraldic symbols varies considerably and sources that explicitly identify each magus with a designated part of the world are nearly non-existent (the traditions concerning their origin do not refer to the continents) (*BE* 491–99).

Nevertheless, Wintle's interpretation draws our attention to an important development: even if the precise identification of the "black magus" remained variable, the ascription of a specific skin colour became widespread towards the end of the

---

**22** Wintle, *Image of Europe*, 191–216.

Middle Ages.[23] In addition, at least one (very peculiar) object does indeed provide a clear identification: around 1460, the Dauphin Louis (later King Louis XI of France), donated a monstrance in the form of a *mappamundi* to the church of Halle, near Brussels. The object's structure was quite extraordinary, and it identified the magi as well as the continents with little metal bands that carried inscriptions on both sides: Balthasar stood for Asia, Caspar for Europe, and Melchior for Africa.[24]

All in all, the three magi were the basis for a broad range of allegorical interpretations, for instance as representatives of the three religious communities of the Jews, the Muslims, and the Christians who would all eventually unite in the Christian church. The motif did not provide a stable tradition to ascribe specific characteristics to the continents and their inhabitants until at least the end of the Middle Ages. It bears witness to an increasing "blackening" of Africa, however, thereby contributing (together with the stories about Ham) to the development of an increasingly racial perspective of the world.[25] This process intensified in the early modern period and ended up providing one of the justifications frequently used for the brutal enslavement of huge numbers of "nonwhite" people.

All these traditions were largely built on a mainly religious foundation. They were complemented by more scientific approaches that partly relied on ancient climate theory: just

---

**23** Michael Wintle, "The Advent of the Black Magus. Moving towards a Continental Hierarchy," in *Order into Action. How Large-Scale Concepts of World Order Determine Practices in the Premodern World*, ed. Klaus Oschema and Christoph Mauntel (Turnhout: Brepols, 2022), 209–35.

**24** Oschema, *Bilder von Europa*, 509 and fig. 41.

**25** For a synthesis on racial perspectives in the Middle Ages, see Geraldine Heng, *The Invention of Race in European Middle Ages* (Cambridge: Cambridge University Press, 2018); cf. Benjamin Braude, "The Sons of Noah and the Construction of Ethnic and Geographical Identities in the Medieval and Early Modern Periods," *The William and Mary Quarterly* 54, no. 1 (1997): 103–42.

as Aristotle had argued for the excellence of the Greeks by referring to the qualities of the space they inhabited—between the extremes of the cold North and the hot South—medieval authors frequently referred to the influence of climates to identify the specific qualities of Europe and, therefore, its inhabitants. One might be surprised to learn, however, that Europe did not always occupy the top of the rankings: according to Gervase of Tilbury's *Otia imperialia*, written in the early thirteenth century, Asia was not only the largest, but also the most beautiful part of the world (*maior et uberior pars*) (part/ *decisio* 2, chap. 2), which explained why Noah's eldest son Shem had inherited it. Japheth's Europe was merely "equally good" (*similiter bonam*), while Ham inherited "the more barren" (*sterilior*) Africa. Combining juridical reasonings (the eldest son inherits the best part), geographic observations (Asia is the largest part), and climate theory (Asia and Europe are good, but the former is the most beautiful), Gervase established a ranking that was quite representative for late medieval authors' opinions. Although the details could vary, most authors would not have denied the excellence of Asia— but they were especially unanimous as far as the disadvantages of Africa were concerned:[26] while Isidore mentioned in his *Etymologies* that the latter at least lacked the "horror of the cold" (*horror frigoris*) (bk. 14, chap. 5, §1), Pierre d'Ailly reverted this assessment when he observed that the cold is easier to endure than heat (*BE* 318). To him, and to many others (not least the makers of the *mappaemundi*), Africa was a largely unknown, inhospitable, and dangerous place, with deserts, venomous beasts and monsters, and inhabited by bad people (as explicitly mentioned by Albertus Magnus). In stark contrast to these negative stereotypes, late medieval authors had very positive things to say about Asia and its riches, which are frequently mentioned. Fazio degli Uberti's *Dittamondo* (fourteenth century) furnishes an excellent example for this: it describes Asia as being as large as Africa

---

**26** See Mauntel, *Asien—Europa—Afrika*.

and Europe taken together and "rich in gold" (bk. 1, chap. 6, ll. 55–63), while Europe brings forth very worthy people. Mandeville's *Travels* concur with this image.

It was not before the mid-fifteenth century that authors began to invert this order and to argue for the precedence of Europe, as for instance Lorenzo Valla (d. 1457): "we attribute this palm to Europe as far as any kind of dignity is concerned" (*ita palmam Europe tribuimus in omni prope genere dignitatis*) (*BE* 450). Being a humanist, his logic was mainly based on ideas of Roman greatness and the value of the Latin language, which had been preserved (and reinvigorated) in Europe, not least owing to the force of the Christian faith.

But which specific phenomena could be attributed to Europe? Most authors seem to have been primarily interested in the size of the continent, its fertility (mainly in agricultural terms, but also with respect to the inhabitants), and moral qualities. While Cyriakus Spangenberg (d. 1604) claimed that Europe was not inferior to the other continents in these regards, some earlier authors picked up ancient traditions to develop a more positive picture: Bartholomaeus Anglicus (d. after 1250), for example, referred in his encyclopaedic *De proprietatibus rerum* to Pliny's *Historia naturalis* in order to make clear that Europe might be smaller than Asia, but was the latter's equal in population size. In addition, it brought forth stronger, hardier, and more beautiful people than Asia or Africa (bk. 15, chap. 50). The importance of this characterization can hardly be overestimated: Bartholomew's text was widely read and copied in the late Middle Ages and his appraisal of Europe's excellence is mirrored in the *Polychronicon* by Ranulf Higden (d. 1364) as well as in Felix Fabri's (d. 1502) *Evagatorium*; indeed, Petrus Apianus still quoted it in the sixteenth century (*BE* 323–24).

This positive characterization, which has a crude racist, Eurocentric overtone to modern ears, was based on climate theory: Europe's fertility could be explained by its moderate temperature, and the same applied to the strength and the braveness of Europe's inhabitants. The colder climate (in comparison to Africa) led to a more excessive production of blood and bodily fluids; as a consequence, the men of Europe were supposedly less fearful of being wounded in battle.

The importance of ancient climate theory for the further elaboration of pertinent arguments in the late Middle Ages can also be seen in Nicole Oresme's works: in the second half of the fourteenth century, Oresme translated several of Aristotle's works into French, furnishing commentaries and explanations. In his comments on the *Politics*, for example, he underlined that the "barbarians" were "by nature" more servile in their habits—and the same applied to Asia in comparison with Europe. He duly stressed that this did not mean that every individual from Asia was more servile than every individual from Europe, but still the former had a "less freedom-loving nature" (*il ne sunt pas de si franche nature*) (*BE* 350). For Oresme, the differences also resulted from the "age" of the respective cultures, an idea that is intimately connected with the motif of *translatio*, implying that the course of history was connected to a geographical movement that led towards the West: the Orient had become "old" in Oresme's eyes (and in those of many others) and thus prone to the destruction caused by bad government and wars. The ensuing effects encompassed all physical and mental aspects of human beings: according to the *Livre de Sydrac* (late thirteenth century), for example, the people from the Occident (*Ponant*) were wiser than those from the Orient (*Levant*), since their brains suffered less from extreme heat (*BE* 354).

It is difficult to gauge whether and to what extent these reasonings are representative of what people believed in the late Middle Ages: impressive as the individual citations are, they were not part of a coherent discourse about the "nature" of Europe but are scattered among different texts. Taken together, they seem to imply that authors from the Latin West became increasingly aware of Europe as a category that could furnish a meaningful frame for their works on history, culture, or natural philosophy. While they express a certain claim to superiority, the number of those texts and passages remains limited.

In sum, the growing presence of the term "Europe" seems to have derived from practical considerations and discussed in pertinent terms: whether Europe was as densely populated as Asia, for example, was not so much a concern *per se*; it was only important because the answer had profound repercussions for the prospects of a new crusade. In most contexts, Europe was not loaded with affective connotations, as is implied by the speeches and bulls of Enea Silvia Piccolomini, *viz.* Pius II; rather, it provided a useful category and framework for the apprehension of the author's own world and for practical solutions to actual problems. Towards the end of the fifteenth century, for instance, Philippe de Commynes announced in his *Mémoires* that he wanted to focus on Europe because this was the part of the world that he was familiar with—which did not mean, as he explicitly underlined, that "they," (i.e., inhabitants of other continents) did not have "wars and quarrels" just as "we" did (bk. 5, chap. 18)! And although Commynes interpreted the politics in Europe as being governed by the antagonisms of God-given competitors, he would probably have claimed the same for the other parts of the world. It was only towards the sixteenth century that authors like Machiavelli elaborated in more detail that Europe was particularly suited to bringing forth "excellent men" (*uomini excellenti*) due to the multiplicity of kingdoms and "republics" that existed here in permanent competition, while Asia and Africa were merely ruled by a small number of large realms (*BE* 431).

In the meantime, the communities that inhabited Europe had developed administration and infrastructure that helped the progressive integration of the different parts of the continent from the thirteenth century onwards. Once again, the Church was a decisive factor: even John Quidort of Paris, who presented the differences between secular realms in his *De regia potestate et papali* (ca. 1302/1303) as a natural and legitimate phenomenon, recognized the ideal of one unified and universal Church. With his ideas on the differences between peoples and the effects on secular rule, he provided a theoretical basis for what historiographers had implicitly practised for a long time: while they didn't hesitate to use the broad designation as "Asians" and "Africans" for populations outside Europe, they usually applied much more precise categories for peoples inside Europe. Hence the anonymous author of a *Tractatus de locis et statu sancta terre ierosolimitane* (ca. 1168/1187) painstakingly noted that the "Latins are divided into various peoples: Germans, Spanish, French, Italians, and other peoples that Europe brings forth" (*Latini etiam in gentes varias dividuntur: Alemannos, Hispanos, Gallos, Italicos et ceteras gentes quas parit Europa*) (*BE* 375).

This idea (and the accompanying practice of reducing the "others" to a simplified unit, while providing details on what counted as "own") did not always take on the elaborate form of a functionally differentiated model like Alexander von Roes's. Nevertheless, the experience of an increasingly entangled and tightly administered continent led to the perception of Europe as being home to a plurality of realms that somehow belonged together (first and foremost for religious reasons). The Roman Church played a decisive role in this: in 1215, the Fourth Lateran Council prescribed a clear model for the communication between the Papal Curia and individual parishes (and vice versa) via intermediary bodies, like regional synods. In 1336, when the papacy resided at Avignon, the Papal Bull *Vas electionis* regulated the organization of the payment of the taxes that were owed to the Curia. The text divided the entire Church into four units: France (and a series of smaller neighbours), the Spanish kingdoms, the Italian provinces (including Greece and the islands of the Mediterranean), and finally a "German" group, that included the Scandinavian kingdoms, Hungary, Bohemia, Poland, and England (*BE* 377).

This model was originally established for fiscal purposes only, but several decades later, the quadripartite structure became prominent in an entirely different context: when the Ecumenical Council at Constance (1414–1418) was assembled to end the Schism that had divided the Catholic Church into two obediences since 1378 (and three, from 1409), the participants decided to organize their deliberations and their votes in four "nations" (*nationes*). This procedure compensated for the overwhelming number of bishoprics in Italy in comparison with the regions north of the Alps, and *Vas electionis* provided an authoritative model. During the Council, a curious conflict arose that sheds light on the increasing importance contemporaries attributed to a structure that organized the space of Europe (and partly beyond): when the Council opened its proceedings, the Spanish kingdoms sent no delegation, adhering to Pope Benedict XIII who refused to submit to the authority of the Council. The participating delegations were thus divided into the four nations of Italy, France, Germany, and England. After the arrival of the Spanish delegation in late 1415, a violent debate arose: should there be a fifth nation? Or should the English henceforth be part of the German nation, as *Vas electionis* prescribed? In the end, the Council chose to recognize a fifth—at a time when England and France were in the middle of the Hundred Years' War, the English would not have accepted becoming part of another "nation," while their adversaries remained "autonomous."

Most interesting for us is that this debate included explicit reflections about the structure of Europe: in order to justify the status of the English, Thomas Polton submitted a *Vindicatio* on March 31, 1417.[27] He suggested that Europe had been divided into four primary kingdoms in ancient times, as could (allegedly) be seen in Albertus Magnus and Bartholomaeus Anglicus (who had never written any such thing): Rome, Constantinople, Ireland, and Spain. Since the role of Ireland had been "transferred" onto England, Polton argued, the latter was now one of the four foremost kingdoms of Europe and deserved its own "nation" much more than France. The treatise also discussed an alternative, namely that Europe had

---

**27** See Robert N. Swanson, *"Gens secundum cognationem et collectionem ab alia distincta?* Thomas Polton, Two Englands, and the Challenge of Medieval Nationhood," in *Das Konstanzer Konzil als europäisches Ereignis. Begegnungen, Medien und Rituale*, ed. Gabriela Signori and Birgit Studt (Ostfildern: Thorbecke, 2014), 57–87; cf. Oschema, "Eine Christenheit," 42–44.

been divided into five provinces or "nations." To further their own position, the English proposed use of the cardinal points of the compass to develop a quadripartite model for Europe: after all, Spain and France would always remain in the West, while England was in the North, etc. At the heart of the problem was the question of the appropriate structure of the Church, or rather of all of Christendom since the Council considered itself to be universal; but possible divisions of Europe served as well.

What does this mean from a broader perspective? In the rest of the Council's debates the notion of Europe played no particularly prominent role, and the central concepts remained the Church, Christendom, and Christianity. While the use of Europe in the conflict about the "nations" suggests that the participants perceived the continent as a relevant entity, its specific context also demonstrates that it was not particularly imbued with any affective value—quite the contrary: the English argument fundamentally relied on the assumption that "nations" would find it unacceptable to be subordinate to other nations, and the structure of Europe furnished a neutral and malleable umbrella.

So, towards the end of the Middle Ages, we find a range of different contexts in which the notion of Europe was increasingly applied. Yet, the use of the term does not suggest one clear meaning dominated: we can merely say that it had become part of many authors' vocabulary, authors who often used it as a self-evident frame of reference. In addition, the notion could be used to appeal to more specific ideas that were occasionally related to religious, cultural, and natural characteristics.

## Description or Ideal?

The broad variety of contexts in which Europe could be used solicits the question of whether the term can mostly be characterized as a descriptive tool or as an instrument of motivation? The example of Enea Silvio/Pius II and others who called for the defence of Europe in order to protect the Church (and ultimately to avoid the coming of the end of time, as George of Trebizond argued),[28] vividly illustrates that the word could become part of political appeals in the broadest sense. This built upon the growing tendency of authors in the Latin West to situate themselves in Europe, not least due to the increasing awareness that this was only one part of a larger world. In this sense, the significance of Europe did not have to rely on its being "special" (even though, as we've seen, some authors believed it to be): its role and its importance were immediately connected with its being just one of the three parts that constituted the *ecumene together*—Europe became meaningful as part of a larger entity.

As self-evident as this might sound, it is a factor that has long been overlooked, for example in analyses of the cartographic material: very few maps that claim to represent Europe as a separate entity have survived from the eleventh to fifteenth centuries. As to the exceptional maps of Europe, one of the most famous of these was authored by Lambert of St. Omer in the autograph of his encyclopaedic *Liber Floridus* (ca. 1120). Lambert depicted Europe separately under the heading *Europa mundi pars quarta* but kept the traditional form: the continent thus appears as a circle-segment that gives the impression of a cut-out (or a zoom-in) of a traditional T–O-map. The author's reason for producing such an unusual map is the subject of ongoing debate: Hartmut Kugler, for example, interpreted it in the context of the crusade-movement, arguing that the map evoked the image of

---

**28** Klaus Oschema, "Ego Europa—die Zukunft eines Kontinents und der Untergang der Welt," in *Die Aktualität der Vormoderne. Epochenentwürfe zwischen Alterität und Kontinuität*, ed. Klaus Ridder and Steffen Patzold (Berlin: Akademie, 2013), 341–72 at 366–69; for George's *Exhortatio ad defendenda pro Europa Hellesponti claustra* see *Collectanea Trapezuntiana. Texts, Documents, and Bibliographies of George of Trebizond*, ed. John Monfasani (Binghamton: Center for Medieval and Early Renaissance Studies, State University of New York at Binghamton, 1984), 434–44.

an open hand, which Kugler identifies as the "hand of God."[29] Lambert might thus have wanted to demonstrate Europe's Christian character. For the moment, however, such interpretations remain hypothetical. What is clear is that he did not merely want to illustrate his textual description of Europe: the map also shows a combination of red lines that seem to outline the Carolingian realm divided into three parts that can roughly be identified with Italy, France, and Germany. Later authors, such as Alexander of Roes, identified these with the most important kingdoms in Europe, but Lambert may have wanted to evoke an historical situation long before his own time of writing. In any case, this extraordinary map did not pique the interest of his contemporaries: while two other twelfth-century copies of the *Liber Floridus* survive, the map of Europe only figures in the author's autograph.

Apart from Lambert's map, only two other maps are known that seem to have been envisaged to explicitly represent Europe.[30] One of these is contained as a separate leaf in a manuscript from ca. 1200 with the works of Gerald of Wales, conserved in Dublin. According to modern geographical standards, the map appears quite strongly distorted, but this observation disregards its maker's intentions: he (or she) wanted to highlight the islands of Britain and Ireland (which figure prominently), as well as their relation to Flanders, France, and finally Rome. Only a few decades later, Matthew Paris included a map in one manuscript of his *Chronica majora* which focuses on large parts of Europe (but cuts off the northern islands) and only crudely renders the North African coast and the Levant. Once again, the motivations for this specific representation are unclear: the accompanying text, rendered in the Asia section, refers to Macrobius and his comment that the *ecumene* had the form of a *chlamys extensa*, an out-

---

**29** Hartmut Kugler, "Europa pars quarta. Der Teil und das Ganze im 'Liber floridus'," in *Europa im Weltbild des Mittelalters*, 45–61 at 55–59.

**30** For this paragraph, see Oschema, *Bilder von Europa*, 468–71 and figs. 12–13.

spread cloak. Matthew claimed that Europe, the "fourth part of the Earth," which he explicitly identified as "our part of the habitable [zone]" (*nostre partis habitabilis*) had a triangular shape.[31] As to the further implications of this observation, the author remains silent, but the individual objects the map represents seem to suggest a focus on Christianity.

The limited number of extant maps of Europe does not imply that Europe did not figure prominently on medieval maps, however: it was a key part of the *mappaemundi* or T-O-maps, and part of the tripartite structure of the inhabited world.[32] Once again, Europe gained its significance from being a part of an overarching structure. A closer look reveals details indicating that mapmakers were not only particularly familiar with this part of the *ecumene*, but that they also wanted to underline its specificity. We have already seen (fig. 1 above) that the Beatus-map from Burgo de Osma used the prominent presentation of the apostles' graves to ascribe a religious role to Europe. Later examples, like the huge Ebstorf map (destroyed in the Second World War, but still available to us through photographs that allow its reconstruction) tend to highlight the presence of roads and cities in Europe, while Asia and Africa (but also the margins of Europe) mostly appear to contain either objects from ancient or biblical history, or miraculous features like the so-called "monstrous races."[33] At least implicitly, these maps convey the impres-

---

31 Oschema, *Bilder von Europa*, 469–70; Daniel K. Connolly, *The Maps of Matthew Paris. Medieval Journeys through Space, Time and Liturgy* (Woodbridge: Boydell, 2009), 166–67.

32 Mauntel et al., "Mapping Continents," 311.

33 For Europe in the so-called Ebstorf-map, see Harald Wolter-von dem Knesebeck, "Der Kontinent der Städte und Wege. Europa und seine Stellung in Welt und Weltgeschichte auf der Ebstorfer Weltkarte," in *Gründungsmythen Europas im Mittelalter*, ed. Michael Bernsen et al. (Göttingen: V & R unipress, 2013), 105–32; for a critical position, see Margriet Hoogvliet, "The Wonders of Europe: From the Middle Ages to the Sixteenth Century," in *Europa im Weltbild des Mittelalters*, 239–55. On the "monstrous races," see

sion that Europe increasingly became the region with which the mapmakers felt familiar, relegating the miraculous and "supernatural" motifs to a position either at the margins or even outside this part of the world.

This cartographic material literally illustrates what late medieval Latin Christian authors associated with Europe on a descriptive level: first, the geographical bounds, quite clearly circumscribed. This frame was then used to identify specific features, whose designation as "the largest" or "the most important in Europe" in turn reinforced the ideas of Europe as a meaningful natural or cultural unit. Most of these references concerned relatively simple features: rivers, cities, peoples (and their origins), etc. More sophisticated aspects that expressed the idea of political or administrative unity, however, remained largely absent—the most remarkable exception was furnished by ideas concerning the administration of the Roman Church. Not only was the Church the only institution that could pretend to a structure that encompassed large parts of Europe (and sometimes beyond) by the end of the Middle Ages; in crucial moments discussions on its politics could also actually refer to the continent, as we could see in the debates on the "nations" at the Council of Constance. During the period in which the popes resided at Avignon (1309–1377) and discussions about their return to Rome ensued, an author like Ansel Choquart not only emphasized that most of the Christians of his time lived in Europe, but also that Marseille was in the centre of the continent, not Rome—thereby arguing for the papacy to remain in Southern France rather than return to Italy.[34]

---

*Medieval Monsters: Terrors, Aliens, Wonders*, ed. Sherry C. M. Lindquist and Asa Simon Mittman (New York: The Morgan Library & Museum, 2018); Rudolf Simek, *Monster im Mittelalter. Die phantastische Welt der Wundervölker und Fabelwesen* (Cologne: Böhlau, 2015), and John Block Friedman, *The Monstrous Races in Medieval Art and Thought* (Cambridge, MA: Harvard University Press, 2000).

**34** Jean-Marie Moeglin, "Hat das Mittelalter europäische lieux de

As far as secular rule was concerned, late medieval authors rarely wished for a powerful ruler to unite the continent under his authority: while the notion of an "Emperor of Europe" (*imperator Europae*) can be found in late medieval texts, albeit infrequently, it basically conveyed the negative idea of external tyrants who might strive for universal power. This idea was mostly a projection and part of the "Othering" of non-Christian rulers outside of Europe, but it was not fiction either. Mongol rulers did, in fact, claim a mandate to conquer and rule the entire world, as thirteenth-century travellers to the East correctly observed, and Sultan Mehmet II's successor Bayazid II explicitly asserted rule over Asia and Europe after the conquest of the imperial city of Constantinople in 1453.[35]

This general disposition did not, however, prevent individual authors from referring to Europe in specific contexts when they wanted to motivate their audience: in the late Middle Ages, the idea of a new crusade continued to occupy the mind of many authors far beyond the fall of Acre in 1291 and the loss of the last Latin Christian territories in the "Holy Land." In the aftermath of this event, numerous crusade treatises were written and circulated that proposed how such an endeavour could be organized.[36] While Europe did not always explicitly play an important role in these texts, many of them shared the conviction that one of the main problems was the internal divisions of Christianity. Several treatises proposed different methods for internal pacification and so provide the basis for successful coordinated action against the Muslims. One of these texts, the *De recuperatione Terre Sancte*,

---

mémoire erzeugt?," *Jahrbuch für Europäische Geschichte* 3 (2002): 17–37 at 24–25.

**35** Oschema, "No 'Emperor of Europe'," 432.

**36** For an overview, see Norman Housley, *The Later Crusades, 1274–1580. From Lyons to Alcazar* (Oxford: Oxford University Press, 1992); several treatises are edited in *Projets de croisade (v. 1290–v. 1330)*, ed. Jacques Paviot (Paris: Académie des Inscriptions et Belles-Lettres, 2008).

was written between 1305 and 1307 by the Norman legist Pierre Dubois, and it proposed the creation of a "League of Princes" that would ensure the pacification of the Catholic Christians who lived between the Occident and Greece. From the mid-twentieth century onwards, Dubois's text has repeatedly been described as a first project of "European unification"[37]—and it did indeed propose fascinating ideas for the institutional organization of a league of sovereigns in the form of a permanent congress with its own means of settling conflicts. However, Dubois was clearly not interested in Europe: not only did he probably think of the "league" as a means of furthering the interests and authority of his own sovereign, the French king Philip IV, he also failed to refer to "Europe" even once. The category at the heart of the project was clearly Catholic Christendom (*catholicos*) or the "Christian Republic" (*respublica christicolarum*) as well as the Roman Church (*ecclesia romana*).

Over a century later, another peace-project with similar traits was proposed by the Hussite king of Bohemia, George of Poděbrady. In the face of Ottoman expansion and a precarious situation, he tried to further his acceptance by the Catholic Church with his proposal. Once seen as heretics (the Bohemian preacher Jan Hus having been burned at Constance in 1415), the Hussites had reached an agreement with the Roman Church at the Council of Basel; however, Pius II had these so-called *Compacts of Basel* annulled in 1462. Poděbrady's project, developed at his behest by Antonio Marini and negotiated with the kings of Poland, Hungary, and France, proposed the creation of a league of princes within which autonomous institutions would provide for the set-

---

**37** See Lotte Kéry, "Pierre Dubois und der Völkerbund. Ein 'Weltfriedensplan' um 1300," *Historische Zeitschrift* 283 (2006): 1–30; on Dubois also Chris Jones, "Rex Francie in regno suo princeps est: The Perspective of Pierre Dubois," *Comitatus* 34 (2003): 49–87. An English translation of Dubois' text is available in *Pierre Dubois: The Recovery of the Holy Land*, ed. and trans. Walter I. Brandt (New York: Columbia University Press, 1956).

tlement of conflicts to allow for the preparation of common defence against the Ottomans. Once again, Europe played no explicit role: although the introductory passages deplored the expansion of the "Turks" in Asia and Africa, the circle of those who were invited to participate was defined in religious terms—the aim was the protection and defence of the "borders of Christendom" (*fines Christianorum*).[38]

It is true that the addressees of both projects comprised many princes that we might situate in Europe from a modern perspective; however we must note that neither Pierre Dubois nor King George chose to develop their ideas in European terms. This does not affect their proposals' originality; it merely means that we must interpret them in their own historical context and take their words seriously.

All in all, we must conclude that the connotations of Europe strongly varied by the late Middle Ages: while some authors proposed highly elaborated ideas about functional cooperation between European realms (Alexander of Roes), others merely used the word in order to distinguish between a part of the world with which they felt most familiar in contrast with the world "outside." Although the latter uses also express cultural connotations, they often remain relatively matter-of-fact, thereby demonstrating how Europe increasingly became a notion that could be used meaningfully in descriptive contexts. At the same time, the use of the term in emotionally charged contexts, such as the reaction against Ottoman expansion, demonstrates that Europe could acquire an additional wider appeal that served to motivate—mostly for the defence of Catholic Christendom.[39] Despite their motivational force, these appeals did not immediately lead to

---

**38** On Dubois' and Poděbrady's projects, see Oschema, *Bilder von Europa*, 382–89.

**39** For analogous observations concerning the notion *christianitas* see now Nora Berend, "The Concept of Christendom. Christianitas as a Call to Action," in *Order into Action. How Large-Scale Concepts of World Order Determine Practices in the Premodern World*, ed. Klaus Oschema and Christoph Mauntel (Turnhout: Brepols, 2022), 71–95.

more elaborate ideas about what Europe could and should look like. The most we can draw from the sources up till the fifteenth century is that a majority of authors agreed that unified secular rule over the continent was not desirable.

Chapter 6

# Perspectives from Outside?
# Byzantium and the Arabic World

The overwhelming majority of authors and texts hitherto discussed have pertained to the "Western European" or "Latin" cultural orbit (though a few examples were written in a vernacular language). This does not mean that the notion of Europe was entirely unknown to non-Latin communities. The Greek and the Arabic-Persian spheres were familiar with the word, since they inherited it from Greco-Roman Antiquity, in contrast to cultures in the further Asian East, where the continental structure did not play any perceptible role in their models of the structure of the world.[1] In order to broaden the "Latin-centric" perspective, let us outline, at least briefly, the developments in neighbouring cultures.

Only a limited number of studies have attempted to analyze the use of the word Europe in medieval Greek sources, so the basis for even a superficial comparison remains sketchy and asymmetrical.[2] Even so, many of the more basic

---

**1** See Mauntel et al., "Mapping Continents" (with numerous bibliographical references); cf. David Max Moerman, *The Japanese Buddhist World Map: Religious Vision and the Cartographic Imagination* (Honolulu: University of Hawai'i Press, 2021); Pierre Singaravélou and Fabrice Argounès, *Le monde vu d'Asie. Une histoire cartographique* (Paris: Seuil, 2018), with a strong accent on modern material; and Hyunhee Park, *Mapping the Chinese and Islamic Worlds. Cross-Cultural Exchange in Premodern Asia* (Cambridge: Cambridge University Press, 2012).

**2** Important contributions include Basileios Karageorgos, "Der

traits of the notion's use in the Latin West can also be found in the Greek world. This concerns primarily the geographical foundations that medieval Greek authors inherited equally. In this respect, the most obvious particularity of the Greek tradition is the presence of Europe in a limited regional sense (i.e., as a means of identifying a territory within Greece). This found its more formalized occurrence in the province Europe, which appears for example in Constantine VII Porphyrogenitus's treatise *De thematibus*.[3] Overall, this more precise and rather technical usage seems to have been less prominent than the more general designation in the well-established triad of Asia, Europe, and Africa (or Libya for the last in most Greek texts).

In recent decades, several studies have emphasized that Greek authors and their texts sometimes express a sense of community between the Greeks and the peoples in the western parts of Europe. While the non-Roman peoples of the north were at first perceived as "barbarians," the Franks, for example, were accepted by Constantine VII in the tenth century as being more or less on a par with the Romans (i.e., the Byzantines), one indicator being the fact that they intermarried. Despite this nascent sense of community amongst Christians, the escalating conflicts between Latins and Greeks from the eleventh century onwards more frequently highlight the differences: the Latins once again became the "barbarians" from the west, especially in such tense moments as the

---

Begriff Europa im Hoch- und Spätmittelalter," *Deutsches Archiv zur Erforschung des Mittelalters* 48 (1992): 137–64; Johannes Koder, "Zum Bild des 'Westens' bei den Byzantinern in der frühen Komnenenzeit," in *Devs qui mvtat tempora. Menschen und Institutionen im Wandel des Mittelalters. Festschrift für Alfons Becker zu seinem fünfundsechzigsten Geburtstag,* ed. Ernst-Dieter Hehl, Hubertus Seibert, and Franz Staab (Sigmaringen: Thorbecke, 1987), 191–201; Ditten, "Bedeutung von ΕΥΡΩΠΕ".

**3** *The De Thematibus ("On the Themes") of Constantine VII Porphyrogenitus,* trans. by John Haldon (Liverpool: Liverpool University Press, 2021), 164–70.

Latin conquest of Constantinople during the Fourth Crusade in 1204.[4]

Only towards the late Middle Ages and in the face of the Ottoman expansion was the common Christian belief once again underscored to argue in favour of mutual assistance. More neutral terms such as "Latins" (*Latinoi*) or "Franks" (*Frankoi*) came to the fore, while the designation "barbarian" was increasingly reserved for people from Asia or Africa as well as for non-Christians in a more general sense. But even in contexts where the community of Christians was highlighted, this collective was rarely framed in explicitly European terms.[5] In this sense, opposition between a "Christian Europe" and a "barbarian Asia" as found in older research is misleading: Greek authors frequently spoke of the "barbarians in Asia," but references to "the Christians in Europe" seem to have remained more or less absent, though Christianity as a common feature of "Latins" and "Romans" (i.e., the Greeks) was frequently invoked.

So, the Greek development mirrors the Western one insofar as the absence of an explicitly political connotation of Europe is concerned. But noticeable differences exist too: we have few examples of world-maps in Greek Byzantium as a medium for the expression of cultural traits ascribed to the continent (the maps in Kosmas Indikopleustes's *Topographia Christiana* from the sixth century are a rare exception and represent a marginal tradition).[6] In addition, the creative uses of Europe in religious and cultural contexts, which we have seen in the Latin West, were either absent or have not yet been analyzed.

A similarly ambivalent picture can be drawn for the different spheres of the Islamic world: in contrast to older positions

---

**4** See Jonathan Phillips, *The Fourth Crusade and the Sack of Constantinople* (London: Cape, 2004).

**5** See Ditten, "Bedeutung von ΕΥΡΩΠΕ," 503–4 (on the basis of Laonikos Chalkokondyles, who mostly uses Europe to designate the European part of the Ottoman Empire).

**6** Wanda Wolska, *La Topographie chrétienne de Cosmas Indicopleustès. Théologie et science au VIe siècle* (Paris: Presses universitaires de France, 1962); cf. Schleicher, *Cosmographia Christiana*, 241–61.

(e.g., Bernard Lewis), which have been severely criticized in more recent contributions by Daniel König, Arabic authors did not ignore the realms and societies in Europe.[7] Their works, especially towards the later Middle Ages, contained an impressive amount of information on phenomena such as the Roman Empire, the papacy, or even individual peoples. However, they rarely used the notion of Europe to convey the idea of an overarching unit in which the peoples of this part of the world were united (beyond the obvious geographical frame). This observation is quite remarkable for several reasons.

First, the Arabic-Islamic authors inherited, like their Latin or Greek Christian counterparts, the well-established idea of a tripartite *ecumene*. So, they were quite familiar with the notion of Europe (*Urufa*)[8] as well as with climate theory and the ideas it provided about the relation between geographical location and the physiological or personal traits of peoples. In comparison to what can be observed in the Latin Christian world, however, Arabic and Persian cartographers and geographers put no strong emphasis on the continental structure. This is particularly perceptible in the numerous and elaborate world-maps produced in the Islamic world that rarely underscore the divisions between continents, tending instead to focus on places and their connections via routes.[9] Only few specimens even mention the names of the continents—a clear contrast to the *mappaemundi* of the Latin Christian world. While both cartographic and geographic traditions, the Arabic-Islamic and the Latin-Christian one, drew on the same heritage from Antiquity, over the centuries they developed quite different features.

---

**7** See esp. König, *Arabic-Islamic Views*; cf. Ducène, *L'Europe et les géographes arabes*.

**8** König, *Arabic-Islamic Views*, 199.

**9** Mauntel et al., "Mapping Continents," 344; see also Andreas Kaplony, "Die fünf Teile Europas der arabischen Geographen: die Berichte von Ibn Rusta, Ibn Ḥawqal und Abū Ḥāmid al-Ġarnāṭī," *Archiv Orientální* 71 (2003): 485–98. More generally on Islamic cartography, see Yossef Rapoport, *Islamic Maps* (Oxford: Bodleian Library, 2020).

A second important observation concerns the different naming practices: Latin Christian sources identified their "other" not infrequently with collective notions like "Africans" or "Asians" (though more precise or more specific categories are not entirely absent), while they tended to use specific names for peoples and groups within Europe. In Arabic-Islamic sources, however, any identification of "Europeans" is almost entirely absent. This does not mean that their authors were more precise: "Frank(s)" (*al-Ifranj*, *al-Faranj*) was used quite indiscriminately for several groups of non-Greek Christians, while the latter were often addressed separately as "Romans" (*al-Rum*). Nevertheless, the names we find in these texts (distinguishing, for example, between Franks and Slavs, but also the Varangians, *al-Warank*, the English, *al-Anqalīsh*, etc.), do not suggest some idea of a global collective for the entire continent. Of course, it was possible to speak more generally of "the infidel" (*al-kuffār*), thus avoiding the use of more precise (albeit sometimes still quite inaccurate) ethnonyms. Still, this practice differed quite radically from the use of "continental" categories in texts from the Latin Christian world.

Beyond Europe and the parts of Africa and Asia that were close to the Mediterranean Sea, the concept of the parts of the world as developed in Greco-Roman Antiquity disappears entirely: Chinese traditions, for example, put the Chinese realm at the centre of the world, and saw it as surrounded by a series of circular spheres with diminishing cultural value the further the region in question was from the centre.[10] A concept of "parts of the world" was quite alien to this perception; however, individual maps did sometimes refer to the Roman Empire (*Daqin* 大秦), the Byzantine Empire (*Fulin* 弗懍), and other distant regions where strange creatures were supposed to live.[11] It was not before the sixteenth century that Jesuit missionaries brought western geographic ideas to the East, includ-

---

10  Mauntel et al., "Mapping Continents," 305–10.

11  Mauntel et al., "Mapping Continents," 326.

ing the designation of the eastern part of the world as "Asia."[12] While the most widespread geo-cultural ideas implied that the people in the farthest west of the *ecumene* were perceived to be relatively "uncivilized," they contribute little to the development of the notion and idea of Europe in the medieval period.

12 Yuming He, "The Entry of Yaxiya/Asia. The (re)construction of Global Geography in Early Modern China," in *Architecturalized Asia. Mapping a Continent through History*, ed. Vimalin Rujivacharakul et al. (Honolulu: University of Hawai'i Press, 2013), 67–80.

Conclusion

# No Roadmap for Europe—
# History, Politics, and the Way
# to Global History

At the end of this brief overview—which has covered no less than an entire millennium!—many questions necessarily remain open, not least what all this means for us today. In recent years, the idea(l) of the nation-state has once again become prominent. So prominent, in fact, that it visibly endangers the accomplishments of a long-term process of political, administrative, and cultural unification in Europe that had and has several objectives—including securing peace between the member states of the European Union (and beyond).

As we have seen, the experience of the World Wars was a major motivation for historians of the post-war period to analyze the Middle Ages in European terms. Several decades after the first pioneering works, the results remain ambivalent: analyses that consciously apply a European framework to medieval history are no longer rare, but many publications still tend to choose the modern borders between nation-states as their frame of reference. As to the more conceptual approaches that seek to analyze the history of the "idea" of Europe, the outcomes are equally hard to gauge. Some of the initial results presented by Fischer, Hay, and others, clearly must be revised: Europe was neither a "rare" notion in medieval texts (especially since it is hard to evaluate exactly how many—or how few—appearances might justify such a qualification), nor was it "purely geographical." The latter insight is of some importance if we want to adequately describe the mental landscape of the people who lived in the period that we call the Middle Ages. In a cultural setting where the material world was interpreted as God's creation and where everything could acquire symbolic value as a representation of the creator's work, the very idea of the "purely geographical" seems out of touch. And while Europe basically never became a clear-cut political concept during the Middle Ages (in this respect Fischer and Hay were certainly right), it still acquired significant and wide-ranging cultural connotations.

But what might the insights into these connotations tell us today? For one thing, they allow us to avoid misunderstandings that often lead to the misuse of history: Charlemagne certainly did not perceive himself as a "European" ruler, though historians and politicians of the mid- and late twentieth century were quite successful in presenting him as such. And Europe was certainly not merely synonymous with "Christendom" for medieval authors, who were quite capable of distinguishing between the religious community on the one hand and the inhabitants of their part of the world on the other. Modern European authors, who write in a world that has been deeply influenced by phenomena like the Enlightenment and secularization, and who point to medieval Europe to justify the allegedly "Christian nature" of the continent and the societies that live there, are representing an ideological position, not the results of historical analysis.[1] As is so often the case, the realities are far more complex—and this history of the notion of Europe, which might not live up to the expectations of some, can serve as a useful reminder of the difference between History and Politics. In short, knowledge about the notion's use in the Middle Ages can tell us about the cultures of the medieval world, but it cannot provide a blueprint for contemporary and future politics.

Although there has been a tendency to construct, for political purposes, a "Christian Europe" justified through historical references, such endeavours, I would argue, are an abuse of what history can and should be. On the other hand,

---

**1** For an excellent critique, see Hasse, *Was ist europäisch?*

this topic is vulnerable to the criticism that it is Eurocentric, which, of course, is true. As we have seen, a "dense" history of the notion of Europe can only be written for the Latin Christian world and, to a certain degree, the Greek world. The use of and interest in the notion was much more limited beyond "Europe," and as far as the Middle Ages are concerned, the history of "Europe" is by and large a European one. This makes it neither obsolete nor antithetical to globalized approaches to the premodern world. On the contrary, detailed and precise analysis of this subject is a necessary piece of the larger global picture of world-order in the premodern world. If we want the Middle Ages to become "global," this piece also has its place—and better knowledge about it might actually contribute to "provincializing Europe" in a quite natural way.

# Further Reading

Bartlett, Robert. *The Making of Europe: Conquest, Colonization and Cultural Change 950–1350*. Princeton: Princeton University Press, 1993.

> Accessible and important outline of central developments that led to the creation of a "European" culture during the Central Middle Ages.

Dawson, Christopher. *The Making of Europe. An Introduction to the History of European Unity*. London: Sheed and Ward, 1932.

> Pioneering work: one of the first studies that explicitly addressed the question of the creation of a "European" culture (mainly identified with the Carolingian realm) in the Central Middle Ages.

Ditten, Hans. "Zur Bedeutung von ΕΥΡΩΠΕ und ΘΡΑΚΗ in der spätbyzantinischen Geschichtsschreibung." In *Actes du premier congrès international des études balkaniques et sud-est européennes. Vol. 6: Linguistique*, edited by V. Georgiev, N. Todorov, and V. Tăpkova-Zaimova, 497–515. Sofia: Éditions de l'Académie Bulgare des Sciences, 1968.

> One of the rare contributions on the notion of Europe in the Byzantine context.

Ducène, Jean-Charles. *L'Europe et les géographes arabes du Moyen Âge*. Paris: CNRS Éditions, 2018.

> Major contribution to the perception of Europe in the Islamic world, with a strong focus on cartographic material.

*Europa—Stier und Sternenkranz. Von der Union mit Zeus zum Staatenverbund*, edited by Almut-Barbara Renger and Roland Alexander Ißler. Gründungsmythen Europas in Literatur, Musik und Kunst 1. Göttingen: V & R unipress, 2009.
> Important collection containing several contributions on Europe and its history in a broad perspective (including the etymology).

*Europa im Weltbild des Mittelalters. Kartographische Konzepte*, edited by Ingrid Baumgärtner and Hartmut Kugler. Orbis mediaevalis 10. Berlin: Akademie, 2008.
> Significant collection with a strong focus on questions of geography (and culture) and cartography.

*Europa-Historiker. Ein biographisches Handbuch*, edited by Heinz Duchhardt, Małgorzata Morawiec, Wolfgang Schmale, and Winfried Schulze. 3 vols. Göttingen: Vandenhoeck & Ruprecht, 2006–2007.
> Very helpful bio-bibliographical reference work on historians who worked on Europe, including a series of medievalists.

*Europäische Erinnerungsorte*, edited by Pim den Boer, Heinz Duchhardt, Georg Kreis, and Wolfgang Schmale. 3 vols. Munich: Oldenbourg, 2012.
> Helpful reference work for a broad selection of important aspects of European history and culture.

Fischer, Jürgen. *Oriens—Occidens—Europa: Begriff und Gedanke "Europa" in der späten Antike und im frühen Mittelalter.* Wiesbaden: Steiner, 1957.
> Pioneering work on the notion of Europe in Late Antiquity and the Early Middle Ages (incl. the tenth century).

Fuhrmann, Manfred. *Alexander von Roes: ein Wegbereiter des Europagedankens?* Heidelberg: Winter, 1994.
> Helpful analysis of Alexander of Roes and his ideas on Europe (including a broader contextualization).

Geary, Patrick. *The Myth of Nations: The Medieval Origins of Europe.* Princeton: Princeton University Press, 2002.
> Significant study that highlights the influence of modern constructs and ideas on the interpretation of historical phenomena, demonstrating how historians contributed to the depiction of the early and Central Middle Ages as the "cradle" of Europe and the nations alike.

Hasse, Dag Nikolaus. *Was ist europäisch? Zur Überwindung kolonialer und romantischer Denkformen*. Stuttgart: Reclam, 2021.

Inspiring and important essay that criticises established approaches and constructions of "Europe" in a historical perspective.

Hay, Denys. *Europe. The Emergence of an Idea*. Rev. ed. of the 1957 original. Edinburgh: Edinburgh University Press, 1968.

Pioneering work on ideas and concepts of Europe, with a focus on the late Middle Ages and the Renaissance.

Heimpel, Hermann. "Europa und seine mittelalterliche Grundlegung." *Die Sammlung* 4 (1949): 13–26.

Pioneering article that demonstrates German medievalists' orientation towards Europe in the post-war period. Holds that the notion of Europe occupied only a minor role in the Middle Ages, but underscores the existence of a "European culture."

Helmrath, Johannes. "Pius II. und die Türken." In *Europa und die Türken in der Renaissance*, edited by Bodo Guthmüller and Wilhelm Kühlmann, 79–137. Frühe Neuzeit, 54. Tübingen: Niemeyer, 2000.

Key study on Pius II/Enea Silvio Piccolomini, his commitment to the organization of a new crusade and his use of the notion of Europe in this context.

Hiestand, Rudolf. "'Europa' im Mittelalter—vom geographischen Begriff zur politischen Idee." In *Europa—Begriff und Idee. Historische Streiflichter*, edited by Hans Hecker, 33–47. Kultur und Erkenntnis, 8. Bonn: Bouvier, 1991.

Well-informed and helpful synthesis of research on and knowledge about the notion and idea of Europe in the Middle Ages, ca. 1990.

*The History of Cartography. Vol. 1: Cartography in Prehistoric, Ancient, and Medieval Europe and the Mediterranean*, edited by John B. Harley and David Woodward. Chicago: University of Chicago Press, 1987.

Collection with helpful contributions for the approaches to Medieval cartographical traditions.

König, Daniel G. *Arabic-Islamic Views of the Latin West. Tracing the Emergence of Medieval Europe*. Oxford: Oxford University Press, 2015.

Fundamental study of knowledge about Europe in the Arabic-Islamic world.

Le Goff, Jacques. *The Birth of Europe*. Originally published in French (2003) as *Europe est-elle née au moyen âge*. Oxford: Blackwell 2005.

Attempt of a major medievalist to outline the characteristics of a European culture, that he sees as an invention of the Middle Ages.

Leyser, Karl J. "Concepts of Europe in the Early and High Middle Ages," *Past & Present* 137 (1992): 25–47.

Helpful overview on much of the Carolingian material in English language.

Mauntel, Christoph. *Asien—Europa—Afrika. Die Erdteile in der Weltordnung des Mittelalters*. Monographien zur Geschichte des Mittelalters. Stuttgart: Hiersemann, 2023 (forthcoming).

Fundamental new study on the role of the continental structure in medieval Latin Christianity.

Mauntel, Christoph, Klaus Oschema, Jean-Charles Ducène, and Martin Hofmann. "Mapping Continents, Inhabited Quarters, and All under Heaven." *Journal of Transcultural Medieval Studies* 5, no. 2 (2018): 295–367.

An attempt to analyze the role of continental structures in medieval cartography in a transcultural and comparative comparison (Latin Christianity, Islam, China).

Mertens, Dieter. "Europäischer Friede und Türkenkrieg im Spätmittelalter." In *Zwischenstaatliche Friedenswahrung in Mittelalter und Früher Neuzeit*. edited by Heinz Duchhardt, 45–90. Münstersche Historische Forschungen 1. Cologne: Böhlau, 1991.

Contribution on the role the idea and notion of Europe in the context of Christian reactions to Ottoman expansion.

Mitterauer, Michael. *Why Europe? The Medieval Origins of its Special Path*. Originally published in German (2002) as *Warum Europa?* Translated by Gerald Chapple. Chicago: University of Chicago Press, 2010.

Recent representative of the attempts to identify and explain the medieval roots of modern European expansion.

Oschema, Klaus. *Bilder von Europa im Mittelalter.* Mittelalter-Forschungen 43. Ostfildern: Thorbecke, 2013.

> Recent synthesis on the notion and idea of Europe in the Middle Ages.

——. "An Irish Making of Europe (Early and High Middle Ages)." In *"A fantastic and abstruse Latinity?" Hiberno-Continental Cultural and Literary Interactions in the Middle Ages*, edited by Wolfram R. Keller and Dagmar Schlüter, 12–30. Studien und Texte zur Keltologie 12. Münster: Nodus, 2017.

> An attempt to analyze and explain the predilection of insular authors (esp. Irish) for the notion of Europe and their influence on continental ideas and uses of the word in the early and Central Middle Ages.

——. "Ein Karl für alle Fälle—Historiographische Verortungen Karls des Großen zwischen Nation, Europa und der Welt." In *Europäische Erinnerung als verflochtene Erinnerung. Vielstimmige und vielschichtige Vergangenheitsdeutungen jenseits der Nation*, edited by Gregor Feindt et al., 39–63. Formen der Erinnerung 55. Göttingen: Vandenhoeck & Ruprecht, 2014.

> Critical analysis of the construction of a "European Charlemagne" by twentieth-century medievalists and its effects.

——. "No 'Emperor of Europe.' A Rare Title between Political Irrelevance, Anti-Ottoman Polemics and the Politics of National Diversity." In "A World of Empires. Claiming and Assigning Imperial Authority in the Middle Ages," edited by Chris Jones, Christoph Mauntel, and Klaus Oschema. Special issue, *The Medieval History Journal* 20, no. 2 (2017), 411–46.

> Focuses on the motif of an "Emperor of Europe" and its use in practices of "Othering" non-Christian peoples.

Schleicher, Frank. *Cosmographia Christiana. Kosmologie und Geographie im frühen Christentum.* Paderborn: Schöningh, 2014.

> Helpful study on cosmological and geographic ideas in early Christianity (Late Antiquity, early Middle Ages).

Schneidmüller, Bernd. *Grenzerfahrung und monarchische Ordnung. Europa 1200–1500*. Munich: Beck, 2011.

> Helpful outline of late Medieval Europe and the growing entanglements with the extra-European world (and their perception).

—— . "Die mittelalterlichen Konstruktionen Europas. Konvergenz und Differenzierung." In *»Europäische Geschichte« als historiographisches Problem*, edited by Heinz Duchhardt and Andreas Kunz, 5–24. Veröffentlichungen des Instituts für Europäische Geschichte Mainz, Beihefte 42. Mainz: von Zabern, 1997.

Important contribution on medieval usages of Europe, proposition to identify the word as "on-call notion," that could flexibly be used in order to motivate against external threats.

Wintle, Michael. *The Image of Europe. Visualizing Europe in Cartography and Iconography Throughout the Ages*. Cambridge: Cambridge University Press, 2009).

Fundamental study on the perception and depiction of Europe, mostly from the perspective of the history of geography, with important chapters on the premodern period.

Printed in the United States
by Baker & Taylor Publisher Services